the
50

GREATEST
ROAD TRIPS
OF THE WORLD

IN ASSOCIATION WITH
TIMPSON

GREATEST
ROAD TRIPS
OF THE WORLD

SARAH WOODS

Published in the UK in 2016 by
Icon Books Ltd, Omnibus Business Centre,
39–41 North Road, London N7 9DP
email: info@iconbooks.com
www.iconbooks.com

Sold in the UK, Europe and Asia
by Faber & Faber Ltd, Bloomsbury House,
74–77 Great Russell Street,
London WC1B 3DA or their agents

Distributed in the UK, Europe and Asia
by Grantham Book Services, Trent Road,
Grantham NG31 7XQ

Distributed in Australia and New Zealand
by Allen & Unwin Pty Ltd,
PO Box 8500, 83 Alexander Street,
Crows Nest, NSW 2065

Distributed in South Africa by
Jonathan Ball, Office B4, The District,
41 Sir Lowry Road, Woodstock 7925

Distributed in India by Penguin Books India,
7th Floor, Infinity Tower – C, DLF Cyber City,
Gurgaon 122002, Haryana

Distributed in Canada by Publishers Group Canada,
76 Stafford Street, Unit 300, Toronto, Ontario M6J 2S1

Distributed in the USA by Publishers Group West,
1700 Fourth Street, Berkeley, CA 94710

ISBN: 978-178578-096-7

Images – see individual pictures

Typeset and designed by Simmons Pugh

Printed and bound in the UK by Clays Ltd, St Ives plc

ABOUT THE AUTHOR

Triple-award-winning travel writer Sarah Woods is a veteran of road-tripping, having driven the iconic 19,000-mile route from North America to South America's tip, completed several dusty voyages in the Australian outback and scaled towering Saharan sand dunes in a 4x4. Sarah has won the prestigious British Guild of Travel Writers 'Travel Guide Writer of the Year' award and has been the recipient of the Kenneth Westcott Jones Award *twice* for thrilling road-trip articles. As a travel presenter on British daytime TV Sarah won the PSA prize for reportage in 2012.

CONTENTS

Africa

Australasia

Asia and the Middle East

The Americas

INTRODUCTION

There is something utterly seductive about the prospect of a road trip. My senses start to tingle at the very thought of hitting the open road, from the preparations and packing up of the car to the unfurling of the map to scrutinise the route and the anticipation of firing up the motor.

Road trips needn't always be long but they should always be scenic in a way that allows the journey to slowly unfold. As the landscape reveals itself and the miles slip magically by, I often feel as if it is the road that is moving – not me and my vehicle. From the driver's seat I have felt every season on my skin through my open window: the warm showers of South America's wet season on the Pan American Highway (see page 225); the bone-chilling cold of Canada's ice fields (see page 189); the deep, rich gold-leafed hues of autumn woodlands along stretches of Tasmania (see page 139); and the stifling airless heat of the desert (see page 163).

Of course, not all road trips are effortless – far from it – but even the most gruelling, wheel-wrenching, gear-crunching slogs hold a special place in my heart. I have learned to view mechanical failures, cavernous potholes and navigational mishaps as part of the entertainment. Wildlife – however big, fierce and reluctant to move – is always exciting company.

As a veteran of unmaintained, roughshod routes I am even tolerant of roadworks and feel any repair works should be welcomed – even those that are poorly timed. My biggest gripe? Gridlocked traffic: the bumper-to-bumper crocodile of cars that is impossible to flee. In *The 50 Greatest Road Trips of the World* I have included only a smattering of routes in which this type of congestion is possible – and all are worth the drive for their glorious hairpin bends and heart-lifting views nonetheless.

Whether you drive for the thrill or for the peace, for the rush or for the space and the thinking time, or simply to get there, this book offers an enticing trip for you all. Settle back and enjoy the ride.

THE 50 GREATEST
ROAD TRIPS

UNITED KINGDOM and IRELAND

PEMBROKESHIRE COASTAL ROUTE, WALES

With over 240 gleaming beaches and a jewel-coloured sea that sends poets into raptures, the secret coves and rugged bays of the Pembrokeshire coast have a knack for capturing hearts and minds. Designated as Britain's only coastal national park in 1952, Pembrokeshire has been rated by the USA's National Geographic *Traveler* magazine as one of the world's top-two coastal destinations. Wild, maritime landscapes have always been a special feature of the 186-mile Pembrokeshire Coast Path, opened in 1970, but since 2012 they are better than ever as part of the 870-mile Wales Coast Path. No other country has created a public footpath that traces its entire coastline. Pembrokeshire's outstanding views across where land, sea and sky meet are enough to make the heart skip. No wonder visitors like me keep returning, year after year.

Road-tripping the Pembrokeshire coastline is to skirt the weather-worn cliffs with one eye on the weather and a neoprene wetsuit, sea shoes and a towel in the car boot. Through the windscreen of my elderly VW Beetle (named Ringo), the views are magical and easily absorbed at a modest 30 miles an hour.

Tucked away in the south-west corner of Wales, Pembrokeshire borders Carmarthenshire to the east and Ceredigion to the north-east. Every part of its coastline is

Photo: Jonesofcam

a heaven for swimmers, beachcombers, wildlife-watchers, outdoor adventurers and walkers – more than 620 miles of public footpaths and bridleways riddle the spectacular coastal scenery around Pembrokeshire's main towns. Rolling green pasture, woodlands carpeted with bluebells and hedgerows bursting with bright yellow gorse. Meadows scattered with flitting butterflies; frolicking dolphins in the sea. Wheeling seabirds screech above the ragged cliffs where seals snooze in the sun. Wild garlic, campion, harebells and cowslips fringe pastoral countryside in a land of constantly changing beauty backdropped by the sea. Few other counties in the UK have anywhere near as many Blue Flag, Seaside and Green Coast awards as Pembrokeshire – with so many wonderful beaches to choose from, the dilemma is where to start.

Driving around the Pembrokeshire coast is a true delight. The road follows cliff-top routes that hug the shore, where seabirds, seals, porpoises, dolphins and whales thrive. Join the route along the coastal waters by taking the A487 south from Newport – it heads through the Pembrokeshire Coast National Park and en route towards St David's passes long salt-water creeks dotted with boats, rock pools and broad curves of golden sand, cave-riddled cliffs and hidden sandy coves and rolling countryside warmed by a milky sun.

Famous throughout Wales for its vibrant community of artists, the small town of St David's is wedged against the country's far south-west coast. As part of the Pembrokeshire Coast National Park, St David's is surrounded by spectacular coastal scenery blessed with an abundance of wildlife. Whitesands Bay, one of the many beautiful beaches in the area, is one of St David's finest and carries the prestigious European Blue Flag Award. Overlooked by the imposing craggy hill of Carn Llidi, this wide expanse of fine white sand curves north towards the remote rocky headland of St David's Head. With pounding surf, roaring waves and blustery cliffs, it has an epic surf 'break' at the northern end. There's a rocky promontory from which to watch the surfers, or at the quieter southern end there are some calmer, sheltered bays. Be sure to study the tides if you plan to swim or relax on any of Pembrokeshire's beaches: the sands you plan to beach-comb may not exist for more than a few hours a day.

As the gateway to the Teifi Valley and the Ceredigion and Pembrokeshire Coast Paths, the ancient town of Cardigan sits on the estuary of the River Teifi at the base of Cardigan Bay. Location-wise, it makes a really good base from which to discover the Pembrokeshire coast.

A delightful little seaside harbour town with cobblestone streets, Tenby is home to some beautiful beaches. Tenby's hilltop position led to its early settlement as a Welsh stronghold, which was replaced in medieval times by a Norman castle and walled town – part of the town walls survive to this day. Fantastic beaches stretch to the north, west and south of the town.

Pembroke Dock, or the Port of Pembroke, grew up around the Royal Navy Dockyard of the early 19th century. Before then, the area was just farmland but by 1901 the town had mushroomed to a population of 11,000. It is here that the Pembrokeshire Coast Path crosses the Cleddau Bridge and passes next to the National Park offices. It then skirts round the waterfront past the Martello Tower on Front Street before heading uphill on the way to Pembroke, where the path has a mellow, leafy character distinctly different from the more rugged coastal stretches.

As the regional 'capital', Haverford West is home to Pembrokeshire's largest congregation of shops, and is an ancient county town built around the Western Cleddau.

Beautiful Barafundle Bay is likened to the Caribbean and is often voted Britain's finest beach – and it is easy to see why. With a hinterland of woods and pastures, and gin-clear waters and sugar-fine sands, Barafundle Bay is remote enough to deter the crowds. The walk down from Stackpole entails a scramble over rocks to reach the moon-shaped bay. Down on the empty sand I spotted a set of lone footprints – an enticing sight that whetted the appetite. Throwing my shoes off to the side, I tiptoed over the sands, sending a few crabs scuttling down into invisible holes as limpid waves lapped the shore.

Contacts:
Pembrokeshire Coastal Route
www.pembrokeshirecoast.org.uk

NORTH COAST 500, SCOTLAND

Scotland's windy coastal road North Coast 500 really does offer road-trippers a chance to 'take the high road' on a route blessed with incredible coastal scenery. New to the scene (it opened in 2014), the NC500 route covers over 500 miles of spectacular Scottish terrain, from Inverness west to the Kyle of Lochalsh, meandering up the west coast, across the rugged north coast to John o' Groats, before heading down the east coast. As Scotland's answer to America's Route 66, the NC500 is aimed squarely at road-trip enthusiasts (cars, vintage vehicles and motorbikes) but has plenty to offer cyclists and walkers. MG sports cars or Harley Davidsons could roar around the route in a long weekend. At a more leisurely pace it could take several weeks to complete, in a loop or in part: beginning and ending in Inverness at Inverness Castle – a landmark of splendour and a fitting location perched atop a hill, overlooking the capital city of the Highlands region.

Keen to delve into rugged rural Scotland? The North Coast 500 extends into the picturesque north-west area of the Scottish Highlands. The route can be driven in a circle – you choose whether you travel clockwise or anti-clockwise: either way takes you to castles, beaches, mountains and numerous attractions. The NC500 website lists everything you pass through or near to on the way – there is also an interactive map and a new NC500 app to help plan your trip.

For drivers who opt to head anti-clockwise, starting at Inverness, head north on the A862 through Dingwall and on to the Black Isle (which isn't an island at all but rather an isthmus 10 miles wide by 20 miles long). Drivers heading along the Cromarty Firth via Invergordon and on to Tain will discover the Black Isle is located in Ross and Cromarty – the NC500 cuts through the hills and coastal areas where there are excellent viewpoints from which to spot dolphins and seals. For 'guaranteed' sightings, take a detour along a topsy-turvy road to Chanonry Point on the Moray Firth, which is hailed as one of the best places in the UK to observe its resident dolphins from the land. North of Tain you cross into the eastern side of the large region of Sutherland, home to the famous eighteen-hole, par 72 Championship Royal Dornoch Golf Course and its velvety fairways and manicured greens. Nearby is the fairy-tale castle of Dunrobin, home to the Earls and Dukes of Sutherland since the 13th century. Its elaborate design and magnificence are a sharp contrast to mile after mile of solitude and space.

Continue travelling further north-easterly and you'll reach Caithness – the famous home of John o' Groats.

Photo: Alancru

As well as the UK's most northerly mainland settlement, Caithness also boasts other attractions such as lighthouse-topped Duncansby Stacks, the furthest point by road, on the north-east coast, from Land's End in Cornwall, being a good mile or two further on than the more famous John o' Groats. This is where the selfie sticks come out, as tourists mark the very tip of Britain with a snap for the photo album.

Keen to learn about the struggles faced by Scottish fisherman who risk life for a daily haul? The former fishing town of Wick reveals a fascinating history: retrace the past at Wick's old harbour and discover the challenges of fishing Scottish waters at the Heritage Museum. There's even a secret harbour far below the headland here − enjoy a brisk walk down the 365 Whaligoe Steps and a heart-pumping upward return journey. Further round the coast of Caithness, the NC500 begins to head west and back into Sutherland, but this time into the wild, raw and beautiful north-western area. Gloriously remote, this region is home to Cape Wrath, the most north-westerly point on mainland Britain, an iconic cornerstone where the north and west coasts of Scotland meet. Pointy sea stacks jut out of a frothy sea, and Orkney can be seen to the north-east and the Western Isles to the south-west. It is a Site of Special Scientific Interest (SSSI) as well as a Special Protection Area for birds; puffins and great skuas nest in its cliffs and rocky ledges. It is, without doubt, one of the most stunning and spectacular of the world's coastlines, with the expansive Atlantic Ocean backed by a vast moorland wilderness. It feels humbling, somehow, as I stare out to sea. There is no land mass between here and the Arctic.

Heading south towards the ferry port town of Ullapool, you cross in Wester Ross, the western watershed of Ross-shire with its long sea lochs and imposing mountain peaks. Loch Ewe, Loch Maree and Loch Torridon in particular create a wide, sculpted shoreline. Steep alpine-style mountain slopes add drama and wonder, with the breathtaking mountain pass of Bealach na Ba a particularly slow climb (requiring a low gear and nerves of steel). This is when the NC500 makes you think of the world's great road trips – the corniche of the Côte d'Azur, the Great Ocean Road, the Pacific Coast Highway and Route 66. High-road thrills and stomach-churning perilous climbs offer plenty of opportunity to drive into emptiness and – sometimes – thin air. But what is special about the North Coast 500 is it has no bypasses, dual carriageways and motorway traffic jams. Ancient rocks, millions – nay, billions of years old – tower like mystical beasts: beguiling, beautiful and bizarre. The entire trip offers incredible views that will keep even the most fidgety of drivers happy.

Stuck for a map? You're not alone – as a new route, maps are scarce. To avoid wrong turnings and doubling back, download a copy in advance of your trip from www.northcoast500.com – it's bang up to date.

CAUSEWAY COASTAL ROUTE, NORTHERN IRELAND

This breathtaking route is a driver's delight. No sitting in traffic here. No idle twiddling with the knobs on the car radio. No, this is a road that is a thrill to drive. Really drive. Once you've left the city traffic of Belfast behind, the road starts to narrow. This is when your fists tighten around the steering wheel. If you're used to cruising six-lane freeways, the rugged road along the Antrim Coast may cause your pulse to race. With its curves, quirks and eccentricities, the mainly waterfront route doesn't just offer craggy cliffs, verdant hills, rocky ledges and windswept sands but views out to the rural coast of Scotland too. Before long, Belfast is a distant memory and the road has tapered to a skinny squiggle. Dramatic twists and turns soon necessitate rapid swerves and clumsy gear changes. Crashing waves and windswept arc-shaped beaches flank the open road. Rogue sea-spray douses the windscreen in a drumming thud, sending the wipers into a screeching frenzy – though it is the scenery itself that is the main distraction. The entire coastal road, from Belfast through to Londonderry, is one of truly incredible natural beauty. With every twist and turn, another stretch of picturesque shoreline unfolds on a backdrop of velvety lush green dotted with tiny stone villages. Another wrench on the gear stick brings yet another involuntary gasp of breath – the beautiful bird-filled Belfast Lough, and Belfast docks where the fateful *Titanic* first set sail from the famous shipyards of Harland & Wolff. Next, the pretty seaside town of Carrickfergus beckons, with its well-preserved 12th-century Norman castle and skies full of seabirds. Larne, the gateway to the beautiful Glens of Antrim, offers a diversion, a brief but beautiful loop, to take in the scenic joys of Islandmagee and net-strewn Portmuck Harbour. Back on the mainland, waterfall cascades gain velocity when rain-clouds are swollen – but even Ireland's wet weather can't dampen spirits on this rapturous drive. Characterful houses and stone-built pubs exude true Irish charm from the roadside as the route wriggles around tight bends and up and down nine glens. The Antrim Coastal Road passes by the foot of each of the nine glens: Glenarm (the army glen), Glencloy (the glen of the hedges), Glenariff (the ploughman's glen, known also as the queen of the glens), Glenballyeamon (Edwardstown Glen), Glenann (glen of the rush lights), Glencorp (glen of the laughter), Glendun (the brown glen), Glenshesk (sedgy glen) and Glentaisie (the glen of Taisie, the Princess of Rathlin Island). Many of the rustic inns en route boast traditional folk music sessions, which are characteristic of the area and part of the lure of Ireland's most convivial watering holes. On Rathlin Island there is the added enticement of a population of a quarter-million seabirds, including kittiwake, fulmar, guillemot, puffin and razorbill. You may also see a dolphin or two frolicking around the bay on the 45-minute ferry crossing to the island (if you've time, be sure to do the trip if you can bear to temporarily leave the joys of the road behind).

Back on the road along the Causeway Coast and you'll soon reach a 79-foot chasm where the Carrick-a-Rede Rope Bridge sways rhythmically in stiff winds. Thankfully, the village of Bushmills – home to the world's oldest licensed whiskey distillery – is just around the corner, should you need a nerve-steadier. The journey out to the magnificent UNESCO World Heritage site of the Giant's Causeway is truly fitting as the prelude to one of Ireland's most iconic symbols. Every few hundred metres, something draws the eye – a wildflower meadow, a bizarre-looking cliff-top rock, soft green rolling hills, a few cotton-wool sheep, a rough sea and wispy grey clouds. Precarious dog-legs prove a test of nerves for the most confident driver – the secret, say the locals, is not to hurry. However slowly you go, you'll always get there eventually, they insist. Few routes allow a rewarding meander at such a leisurely pace (no rush: the road will still be there in the morning). A scarcity of traffic and the companionship of the vast, wild ocean and vocal winds ensure the 120-mile journey is a heart-stopping ride.

Many drivers admit to shedding a tear when they reach the Giant's Causeway as it means the lion's share of the

Photo: Tony Webster

driving is at an end. The route, in fact, continues to weave in tight curls all the way to Londonderry. Yet I defy any road warrior not to be wholly cheered by the sight of the Giant's Causeway. Few geological oddities in the world can deliver pure natural theatre on such a mesmerising scale, from the dark stone lapped by brooding waters and jaw-dropping wave-carved rock formations lashed by pounding waves. This magical rocky outcrop is composed of a curious collection of needle-thin columns and spiny fingers – the only such site in Northern Ireland. Ships from the Spanish Armada once floundered off the coastline and little wonder. Recovered treasures from the galleon *The Girona* are on proud display at the Ulster Museum in Belfast. Not that you'll give this a thought as you survey this fairy-tale landscape of hidden islands, coves and rocky caverns. For you may well be preoccupied by the whereabouts of a local giant called Finn: some say that they have witnessed the giant, who wears a size 47 shoe, disappearing through a concealed doorway in the rock face. It is believed that deep below, set within the cliffs, a vast chamber offers a place where a giant could enjoy uninterrupted sleep. Archaeologists, historians and giant experts converged on the scene after news of the incident spread, but despite rumours of 'the unmistakable sound of snoring' there were no sightings. According to the locals, all mythical creatures – giants, leprechauns and elves – hibernate during winter, so the best chance of eyeballing this former warrior is to visit once he's woken up in spring and the warmer months.

The route to Londonderry passes through villages and countryside scattered with sheep to the romantic ruin of Dunluce Castle, then on through Portrush and Portstewart before the Causeway Coastal Route heads towards Limavady, via Castlerock. If you can tear your eyes off the demands of the route, be sure to scour the cliff-tops for the glorious Mussenden Temple, a handsome folly inspired by the Temple of Vesta in Rome, Italy. The road begins to widen the closer you get to the walled city of Londonderry – the only entirely wall-encircled city in the British Isles. With its lively music, comedy and arts scene, this is the place to visit off-the-wall galleries, recitals and clubs in among its historic streets and 17th-century walls.

RING OF KERRY, IRELAND

The scenic Ring of Kerry drive brings road-trippers the delights of Ireland in a nutshell. For around the Iveragh Peninsula in south-west Ireland, this 179-kilometre (111-mile) circular route takes in rugged beaches, verdant coastal landscapes, green pasture, medieval ruins, seaside fishing villages and a rocky island topped by a handsome monastery. Ireland is a great country for a road trip and the Ring of Kerry is so full of scenic riches it is almost surreal. Though it can be driven in a day, most people base themselves in Killarney and relish the prospect of exploring 'The Ring', as its splendour gloriously unfolds, over a few days or a week.

From Killarney, the Ring of Kerry can be driven anti-clockwise, towards Kilorgling (the home of Puck Fair, the oldest traditional festival in Ireland), or clockwise, through the gorgeous Killarney National Park towards the walking, trekking and horse-riding country of Kenmare. I chose to head to Kenmare, to avoid the queues of tour buses that have to drive the anti-clockwise route because of the narrow roads. (I'd rather take my chances coming face-to-face with

a tour bus barrelling towards me on a blind corner than be drearily stuck behind it, unable to see a thing: Killarney National Park boasts the most stunning scenery and it would be an absolute crime to miss it.)

Spectacular rocks, shimmering lakes and mountain peaks in Killarney National Park meet thick, inky-green forests – it's a beautiful 30-kilometre (18-mile) drive to Kenmare that makes the heart sing. In Kenmare, pick up the Ring of Kerry to Sneem and then follow it on towards the coast to Castlecove. If you've time, take the steep winding route to Staigue Fort for a hair-raising drive up to the rock-built fortifications through roads as skinny as string. The stretch to Caherdaniel is renowned for its dazzling beach views and they are every bit as magnificent as I'd been told: pale-gold sands and a sea the colour of sapphires set against emerald-green cliffs. Bridle-ways and footpaths loop the cliffs with views through flower-filled meadows down to soft sand. Here, in one of Ireland's Gaeltacht regions where the Irish language remains in daily use, it is as if the crashing Atlantic waves have their own dialect. Soaring peaks and a ribbon of country roads weave through rolling pea-green meadows that have a myriad of trails for horses. To take a break from the car, I arranged to ride a fine Irish steed to sightsee part of the Atlantic Way from the saddle. Renowned for their stamina, versatility and gentleness, Irish horses are famous as proud, dependable and companionable, from the tall, placid Irish Draught and the spirited, intelligent Connemara to the energetic Irish Hunter, the elegant Piebald and the surefooted Irish Cob. Little wonder Ireland's equine tradition has earned it the name 'Land of the Horse'.

The Iveragh Peninsula can be ridden in an hour, half-day or full-day trek and there are several highly reputable stables nestled in the undulating countryside. Fossil-ridden hillsides, ancient stones and ruins are just some of the fascinating sights to be enjoyed. I hoped that my sojourn in the saddle would blow away some cobwebs, as I passed heather-clad hillocks, bird-scattered marshes and juicy pasture. My guide was a wind-weathered veteran of Irish horsemanship who now leads hacks for tourists through this fairy-tale land. I enjoyed a short cross-country canter through Ring of Kerry scenery denied to buses and cars, so I felt especially privileged. My horse of legendary Irish stock and I enjoyed instant camaraderie as we trotted through a meadow flecked with yellow flowers. Sculpted peaks, eerie crags and knotted trails dictated a gentler tempo so we ambled along enjoying Peninsula views of a rich, luminescent shade of green. If you're keen to sightsee in the saddle, seek out A.I.R.E. (the Association of Irish Riding Stables) accreditation, Fáilte Ireland (The National Tourist Board) affiliation and membership of Equestrian Holidays Ireland for the ultimate horse-riding holiday pedigree. Most operators offer a range of handpicked horses to give riders a choice of breed, temperament, colour and size. Equipment and tack is part of the package (although you may prefer to pack your own worn-in helmet and boots) with rides ranging from steady treks along level trails to full-on exhilarating shoreline gallops before cooling off in the waves.

Back on four wheels, and magnificently windswept, the colour in my cheeks and the gleam in my eyes was one of invigoration. From Caherdaniel, I followed the signs to Waterville, a pretty town that forms the gateway to the 18-mile Skellig Ring – a picturesque route to explore if you've the time. From here, the route continues north through resplendent scenery up to Cahersiveen, Kells, Glenbeigh and up to Killorglin – a stretch of the Ring of Kerry likened to Tasmania in Australia with its rugged landscapes, rain-drenched lushness and beautiful beaches. This part of the Wild Atlantic Way is also the route for the Ring of Kerry Charity Cycle (every July) and is also home to the world's best long hike trail (210 kilometres/130 miles) – the Kerry Way. Mile for mile, there is a colossal amount of scenic wow from the mountainous spine that forms the geological backbone of the region, from its translucent glacial lakes and quaint stone-built Irish villages to the rolling green pasture, gigantic rocks and tumultuous Atlantic waves. Whichever way you do it – on foot, by bike, on horseback or in a car – the Iveragh Peninsula is a traveller's joy. Road-trip in summer to make the most of the extended daylight hours to allow you to pootle along at an idle pace in the style of the laid-back locals.

SNAKE PASS, UNITED KINGDOM

As the name suggests, the Snake Pass writhes like a serpent tight against the Peak District's ragged stone ledges. With its superb scenery and far-reaching views across the Pennines and parts of Derbyshire, Staffordshire and Cheshire, the Peak District spans over 555 square miles (1,437 square kilometres). Reaching 1,680 feet (510 metres) at its highest point, the route's biggest thrill after a roller-coaster climb is the long twisting descent into Glossop. On a clear day, views extend to the metropolis of Manchester and beyond.

As the shortest route between two of the UK's northern powerhouses, Manchester and Sheffield, the Snake Pass is part of the region's rich heritage. There had been a road of sorts there since the Iron Age – or earlier. But the Snake

Pass was a specially engineered route by Thomas Telford. The existing roughshod road needed to be upgraded, properly constructed and reinforced, and was opened in 1821 during the Industrial Revolution. Massive advances were being made UK-wide in terms of infrastructure, with canals, bridges, tunnels and railways all playing a part. Travel in this era revolved around packhorses, turnpike roads and coaching inns. Sheffield plate, steel and cutlery made in smoke-spewing foundries were in demand all over the country. Horses – kings of the road for well over 2,000 years – transported these goods out, bringing back commodities such as salt by return. Exports to America were booming and goods had to be carried faster and to sea ports for overseas shipment.

Snake Pass was built as a single stretch of road without any junctions, carved into the rock and climbing in a rising spiral. Cutting across moorland and rough grazing country, with regular milestones, it was touted as a money-saving short-cut. Cargo wagons travelled an average of 2 miles an hour; passenger wagons were speedier at 3 miles an hour (enough to cover 40 miles a day with a regular change of horses). In 1825, Royal Mail coaches were introduced, which had priority on the roads and achieved 12 miles an hour. The guards were armed with blunderbuss, pistols and cutlasses to protect against highway robbery.

Today, it is the scenery that steals your breath away with its beauty – or sheer fright. The unnerving twists, rapid elevation changes and adverse cambers are tricky to navigate with ease. Notwithstanding that, it is a road that should appear on every driving enthusiast's bucket list, even though nowadays there are safer routes. Speed traps, bleating sheep gone walkabout, cyclists and hill-climbers are common hazards on this serpentine way. High accident rates

Photo: Alan Murray-Rust

Photo: Tom Courtney

have forced traffic on 'The Snake' to slow down, allowing full absorption in the majesty of the landscape, rather than missing it in a blur between bends.

As a road number, the Snake Pass is the plain old A57: a sleek, slippery asphalt road that is highly susceptible to flooding, ice and a build-up of snow. It is often closed due to subsidence. Choose from two routes to reach the summit: from Ashopton or from Glossop. Starting from Ashopton, the ascent is over 8 miles (14 kilometres) long with an elevation gain of 991 feet (302 metres) over this distance. From Glossop, the ascent is over 4 miles (7 kilometres) long with an elevation gain of 362 metres (1,188 feet). Snake Pass is one of only a few road climbs in the UK that are comparable in length and average gradient (approximately 7 per cent for around 3.2 miles (5.1 kilometres) to those used in continental cycle racing. For this reason it has frequently featured in the Tour of Britain and is a popular training ground for professional cyclists with their eye on a Yellow Jersey. 'The Snake' as the locals know it, divides local communities: people have either driven it or are too terrified to try. Some leave it until late in life to conquer their fear and drive it. According to a survey conducted by sports car manufacturer Caterham Cars, the 'Snake Pass' section of the A57 tops the list of dream drives, describing it as offering motoring thrill-seekers '25 miles of tarmac roller-coaster'. And as it slices through bleak tufted moorland, rolling hills, pine trees, heather, bracken and babbling streams high above a plummeting valley, it is certainly a 'seat-of-your-pants' type of drive. The weather famously snaps from one thing to another up on the Snake Pass, so it pays to pack good footwear, de-icer, warm blankets, a torch and waterproof clothing since cloud can descend and conditions can become treacherous even on a summer's day. When two Sabre F-86 jet fighters, XD707 and XD730, of RAF 66 Squadron crashed not far from The Snake on their return to RAF Linton-on-Ouse near York in 1954, the wreckage wasn't found for several days due to severe weather. Today, what is left of the crash site can still be seen – fragments of aircraft debris are spread across the moors.

Another historic site is Cutthroat Bridge, a popular walking spot. Named for a gruesome history, the bridge near Ladybower Reservoir is steeped in tales of gore and murder. Cutthroat Bridge was built in 1821, the same year as Snake Pass. Shortly after, a man was found nearby covered in blood with a gash across his throat: he was alive, but died two days later. In more recent times, a decapitated body was discovered in the undergrowth here: a truly horrific find. Thankfully the bridge redeems itself with a sense of calm these days, together with some peaceful moorland views. Spot grouse bobbing up and down in the wild-looking scrub, lizards basking on rocks by the stream, and frogs spawning in tiny pools.

Be sure to stop for traditional British grub at the Snake Inn, also dating back to 1821: a rare place to stay and eat along this wilderness stretch. The Snake Inn is said to get its name from the family emblem of the Duke of Devonshire, a snake in the form of a knot. However, when it was first built, the inn was known as Lady Clough House owing to its location. This fine old hostelry continues to claim its place in history as a vital staging post on the turnpike, half-way between Glossop and Ashopton. Now signed as the 'Snake Pass Inn', it sits right on the A57 with stunning views over the High Peak. Where once it offered stabling for the resting and changing of tired horses, the Snake Inn now has an expansive car park for all the road-trippers – car-drivers, motorbikers and cyclists alike – who stop for roast beef, steak and ale pie or fish and chips.

Contacts:
Derbyshire Tourist Board
www.visitderbyshire.co.uk

EUROPE

RING ROAD, ICELAND

Encapsulating some of the world's most stunning landscape features, Iceland is dubbed the Land of Fire and Ice on account of a unique geo-thermal volcanic and glacial terrain. It looks almost supernatural with its bubbling pools, brackish steams, spouting geysers, fjords, lava caves, volcanoes and black-sand beaches, not to mention dazzling Northern Lights. Crags, chasms, twisted rocks and mammoth boulders characterise the Ring Road's untamed splendour: an unreal landscape studded with gullies and jutting spits of black rock and sparkling gin-clear glacial lagoons. Also known as Route One, or Highway One, the Ring Road loops over 1,330 kilometres (820 miles) right around the island and connects most of Iceland's remote and inhabited corners. Some of the country's most popular tourist sights are reached via this national road, such as the cascading waterfalls of Seljalandsfoss and Skogafoss. Yet it is the eerie calm of Jökulsárlón, a tranquil glacier lagoon about 370 kilometres (230 miles) east of Reykjavík, that draws many people to this route. With its surface at sea level, this glacial lake is a recent addition to Iceland's greatest natural wonders: the result of a warming climate. Ear-splitting creaks fill the air when a mammoth chunk of ice starts to split away from the glacier, Breiðamerkurjökull. There is then a thunderous roar as several tons of ice crack off and pound the water below. As the deepest lake in Iceland at 250 metres (820 feet) deep, Jökulsárlón can accommodate the giant floating frozen boulders as they drift slowly on a four-or-five-year journey that eventually leads to the sea. Warmer temperatures have seen the glacier in this region recede about 20 kilometres (12 miles) since records began and the lake is ballooning in size as the glacier continues to break down. Strolling along the sand beaches on the shoreline, views encapsulate the huge blocks of ice that have drifted out of the lagoon's mouth – a strange sight. Tourist attractions have sprung up around the shores of Jökulsárlón and snowmobiling and ice safaris are popular ways to sightsee the mist-shrouded glacial waters and brooding ancient lava beds. Gaping underwater chasms, filled with gin-clear water from the melted ice, boast such clarity that they shimmer and glitter like cut-class in its purest form. The terrain is surreal: other-worldly and space-like with its eerie moans, penetrating silence, luminous blue icy depths, dreamy weightlessness and shafts of yellow sun. Unsurprisingly, this extraordinary and mystical ice kingdom is often sought by film crews for movie locations, TV commercials and pop music videos – you can see the glacier in all its glory in *Lara Croft: Tomb Raider*, when Angelina Jolie's character was allegedly deep in the frozen tundra of Siberia. It was here, too, that the mythical land of Westeros was recreated for *Game of Thrones*: a wild, mystical and dramatic stage for the land where seven noble families fight for control. It also provided *Star Trek* with the perfect backdrop for one of the key scenes in the 2013 film *Into Darkness*, in which stark volcanic black beaches depicted a bleak, haunting land.

Photo: Borvan53

Drivers will need their wits about them on squiggly curves, blind summits, single-lane bridges and skinny passes where powerful gusts of freezing wind can make every twist and turn hazardous. You're unlikely to achieve speeds of anything much over 40 miles an hour – progress is slow as you skirt around gnarled rocks, fossilised molten lava, charred trees and shimmering lakes. Route One was completed in 1974 to coincide with the 1,100th anniversary of Iceland's settlement. However, about 30 kilometres (19 miles) of the Ring Road's total length still remain unpaved, so make sure your seatbelt is pulled tight and prepare for a rollicking ride across rough stones. Glaciers cover almost 10 per cent of Iceland and ice caves can be found in several locations, but some of the most magical are those reached from Jökulsárlón. To enter an ice cave, you'll need an experienced local guide to navigate the slippery ledges, moving ice and lethal shards of ice: the best months to explore are the coldest months, November to March. With vast areas of Iceland unchanged since the formation of the island, around 16 to 18 million years ago, constructing Route One has been a major milestone. Though the roads, bridges, viaducts and tunnels are, of course, a triumph, they are totally eclipsed by the compelling natural terrain that they traverse. So the actual road you follow is totally overlooked, forgotten and ignored – and quite rightly so.

Boat trips also transport passengers out to sail among towering (and terrifying!) mounds of drifting ice. From open-top amphibious vessels, you can clearly see the subsurface magnitude of these 1,000-year-old ice cubes. Some are as large as islands, others the size of a large armchair. Many are way too big to measure and are home to colonies of seals – listen out for the barely audible splash as they slip into the depths. Tours are comprehensive and tend to be full of facts on the geology, history and ecological fortunes of the lagoon; they are also frequent, running every 30 minutes (or more frequently in high season, June to August).

Contacts:
Jökulsárlón Glacier Lagoon
http://icelagoon.is

Iceland Tourist Board
www.visiticeland.com

ATLANTIC OCEAN ROAD, NORWAY

It pays to get an early start to drive Norway's famous Atlantic Ocean Road (Atlanterhavsvegen), a stretch of Road 64 in between the towns of Molde and Kristiansund. Fierce winds batter this strip of scenic west coast on a daily basis, ensuring that every vehicle that traverses the route is at the mercy of the elements. Powerful waves bash the rocks with relentless force year-round while, in winter, freezing bullets of rain slam against the asphalt. The weather can change in an instant, making journeys near-impossible to plan, and the pounding sea-spray often causes significant damage to passing cars once the skies turn ugly. Flood waters rise – fast – as even the most robust barricades are impotent when the western coast experiences heavy torrents. A true test of driving skills separating the men from the boys sees the Atlantic Ocean Road hailed by Norwegians as one of the world's best holiday road trip routes.

With its seductive curves, Norway's picturesque Atlantic

Ocean Road looks deceivingly slick and smooth for an unsheltered strip of North Atlantic coastline. Draft plans for the Atlantic Ocean Road in the early 20th century included a railway line that would carry eight-carriage trains right across the sea. Unfortunately, the project was quickly abandoned as plans evolved. Today it forms part of Norway's ground-breaking eighteen-road project along the coast and the mountains, combining Norwegian architecture with the spectacle of nature in a design that enhances rather than obstructs the truly heart-stopping scenery. Called the National Tourist Routes (NTR) initiative, the project certainly achieves its objectives along the Atlantic Ocean Road where the construction and natural wonders together have created something greater than the sum of their parts. In total, the NTR cover 1,850 kilometres (1,150 miles) and took close to two decades to complete at a cost of hundreds of millions of kroner.

From Kristiansund, drive through the Atlantic Tunnel to Averøy and then follow signs towards Molde. You know you're nearing the Atlantic Ocean Road when it is way-marked 'Atlanterhavsvegen' in Norwegian. Don't make the all-too-common mistake of following Sat Nav suggestions for alternative stretches – these skip the Atlantic Ocean Road altogether, so you'll miss out on the incredible swoops, dips, sweeping arches, straddling causeways and ambitious swirls battered by brutal seas. Officially, the Atlantic Ocean Road starts at Utheim on Averøya, close to the little village of Kårvåg.

According to Scandinavian drivers' polls, the Atlantic Ocean Road (sometimes also referred to as the Atlantic Highway) has a favourite stretch. You'll instinctively know where on that bit of the road, as it requires no signage. No map or GPS coordinates. No grand fanfare. Suddenly, the route zigzags sharply across a slalom series of eight low bridges that jut out over the ocean. The sea – proud and mighty – seems to almost challenge the idea of the road entering its domain: waves rise up during storms as Man claims the space from Mother Nature. Landfill and salty sea-spray span the distance between the islands to provide a causeway-connected archipelago with wild, transfixing views. A panorama of fjords – intensely coloured in jewel-tone blues and emerald greens – form a dramatic contrast to the chalk-white and silver of the mountains. Your chest tightens a little and your heartbeat quickens as you traverse this roller-coaster road, but with the end in sight you find yourself slowly beginning to exhale. Check your face in the rear-view mirror now and you'll see a smile as wide as an over-stretched hammock. Little wonder the Atlantic Ocean Road is a highly prized 'Norwegian Construction of the Century' – since it was built in the 1980s, the route and its eight breathtaking bridges have become one of the country's most popular tourist attractions. When construction began in August 1983, progress was hampered by no fewer than twelve hurricane-strength storms before the road finally opened six years later on 7 July 1989.

Today, the most famous, and much-photographed, bridge is the Storseisundet. Known locally with fondness as 'the drunk bridge', due to its unusual lopsided lean, it arcs high over the sea at a dizzying angle and is an absolute blast to drive. Another interesting facet are the extra-tough fishing bridges that run either side of the road on the Myrbaerholmbura stretch. Hardcore fisherman hold out here for the cod and mackerel that pass by on the tidal flow, and are, unsurprisingly, drenched to the skin.

Feeling brave? Then open the window while you drive alongside the windswept seas to feel powerful spritzes bouncing against the skin of your cheek. Look out on waters

Photo: Ernst Vikne

rich in cod, cawing seabirds and magical blue-grey bubbly skies. To heighten the mood, switch the radio off and feel the engine moving in rhythm to the atmospheric maritime soundtrack of the Atlantic Ocean Road – a real road-tripping buzz. Such joy and elation is testament that iconic routes don't need to clock up vast distances. The road is only 5 miles long, but boy is it EPIC. With ruffled hair, rough-salt lips and a euphoric sense of wonderment I was left wanting more. Powerless, I couldn't resist the urge to spin the wheel right around to do the reverse journey. Then I crossed the coastal edge of Norway again. Over again. And over again and again.

Contacts:
Atlantic Road website
www.theatlanticroad.com

THE BOLLENSTREEK ROUTE, HOLLAND

From the moment the first tulip was planted in Dutch soil, in 1593, the Netherlands has been a riot of floral colour, with the Dutch in thrall of fragrant, velvety blooms. It is hard, now, to imagine that the tulip isn't native to the Netherlands. Today, Holland's history is inextricably linked with sweet-smelling horticulture, with the tulip at the forefront of it all. Today more than 109,000 hectares (269,345 acres) of fertile lowlands are a carpet of delicate blooms. Holland offers road-trippers a heady springtime drive when the region's fields of tulips, hyacinths and daffodils are at their most splendid. Intoxicating scent fills the air as Mother Nature sprinkles the route lightly with her fine, natural perfume.

Arrive anytime from early April until the end of May to set off along the 40-kilometre (25-mile) Bollenstreek Route for never-ending kaleidoscopic glory that earned it the title 'Drive of a Lifetime' from *National Geographic*.

Haarlem, the capital of the province of North Holland, is the town at the northernmost point of the Bollenstreek Route (sometimes called Bloemen Route or the 'Flower Route'), which runs south to Leiden. Across this region, the soils are rich and full of nourishing organic matter, a result of its history of flooding. Today, dark black soils are irrigated by the surrounding waterways as well as groundwater running beneath the surface. The region has a mix of sandy soils under forest and agriculture, clay soils and peat soils enriched by sediment. Low-lying super-smooth roads, built to sit atop the level lowland fields, occasionally suffer from partial erosion due to a heavy annual rainfall. Follow the route south, along a neat asphalt stretch, and you'll reach a dense concentration of flower fields within a few minutes. The brilliance of the hues is astonishing. Tall, proud tulips in vibrant orange, pink, purple and red; hyacinths with their bubble-shaped blooms in lilac-blue and alabaster white; elegant narcissi and bold, bright yellow daffodils. Planted to form a blaze of colour in alternating strips and contrasting tufted squares, this stunning floral tapestry stretches far into the distance. This incredible non-stop floral extravaganza starts as early as late January, when the first crocuses force their shoots through the soil. Next to make an appearance are daffodils and hyacinths. Then, in early May, irises and tulips start to emerge followed by gladioli, dahlias and fragrant lilies. Set against an expansive sky of breathtaking blue, the Bollenstreek Route is a feast for the senses from the car window: you have a front row seat in a dazzling floral show.

Photo: Lars Plougmann

Head south on highway N208 towards the quaint town of Lisse, famous as the home of the Keukenhof Garden (Stationsweg 166a, Lisse) – a true showstopper on the Flower Route. This spectacular garden started as the small kitchen plot of a 15th-century countess but is now planted to showcase the art of Dutch bulb growers. Stretching across 32 hectares (79 acres) of wooded parkland, the garden is cut with 14 kilometres (9 miles) of walking trails that weave around ponds, pavilions, greenhouses, flower beds and a windmill. To achieve deep, textured and dazzling displays, growers plant more than 7 million bulbs in a trio of layers – the results are mesmerising. Gorgeous blooms fill every available patch of land as far as the eye can see.

From Lisse, continue south on the N208 to highway A44 to reach the sleepy town of Leiden, a historic settlement that is renowned for its picturesque Botanical Garden. Planted in 1594, the garden is subtle and understated – but still contains a dizzying variety of plant species. The route from here is lined with public gardens, special floral events and museums that pay homage to Holland's horticultural tradition. Many private gardens in the villages you pass throw open their doors to visitors – look for the make-shift signs and take a stroll past charming flower beds and floral archways.

A half-hour drive south of Leiden, via the A4 and then the N222, is the pretty town of Naaldwijk. Set in a sea of tulips, hyacinths and daffodils, it denotes the end of the route. Sitting in the middle of the Westland, the world's largest greenhouse area, Naaldwijk is abuzz with wholesale buyers, plant retailers and flower exporters keen to snap up the finest blooms at the largest flower auction in the world. Unsurprisingly, Naaldwijk has one of the highest pollen counts too – so hay fever sufferers beware!

Trains to Haarlem depart from Amsterdam's Centraal

Station at least twice an hour and make the 19-kilometre (12-mile) trip west in less than 30 minutes. There are plenty of places to stay and to rent a car in Haarlem's historic centre: a beautiful town seamed with canals, it is famous for its community of artists and sculptors. Try to drive the route on a weekday as it is popular with domestic tourists, as well as cross-Europe traffic at weekends, when the cyclists are also out in force. Flower sellers set up bloom-filled stalls that form a varicoloured string along the roadside. Eye-popping garlands in a zillion primary hues are snapped up by road-trippers keen to decorate their vehicles, from cars, vans and buses to cycles, scooters and motorbikes.

Contacts:
Bollenstreek
www.bollenstreek.info

Netherlands Tourist Board
www.holland.com

NÜRBURGRING TRACK, GERMANY

As joint-host of Germany's thrilling Formula One schedule, Nürburgring is synonymous with open-wheeled 300-kilometre-an-hour auto racing at 5g pull. Attracting the *crème de la crème* of the motor world's cutting-edge design and world-class electronics, aerodynamics, suspension and tyres, Nürburgring's podium boasts a star-studded winners list. Jackie Stewart, Stirling Moss, James Hunt and Niki Lauda are just a few of the stadium's alumni in a country renowned as the birth-nation of Porsche and BMW, two of the most prestigious high-performance models on the planet. In recent years, Germany's racing heritage has been bolstered by Michael Schumacher, who holds the record for having won the most Drivers' Championships (seven). As the first German winner, Schumacher is credited as the dynamo behind the popularisation of the sport in his homeland. Today motor racing is so popular that Nürburgring now offers diehard fans from all over the world the ultimate thrill: to speed around the Grand Prix circuit in white-knuckle laps from pole position.

Petrol heads from every corner of the globe descend on Nürburgring like a swarm of high-speed ants. Many, like me, are in their own set of wheels. I've driven a Nissan GTR to Nürburgring from England – across the Channel by ferry, then on to Dunkerque (A16) and Lille before heading to Brussels (A10), making sure to avoid the infamous Brussels Ring Road. Once you approach Brussels, look for a service-station on your right (last fuel for a while) and some overhead gantry signs immediately after it. This is your signal to start moving to the right – stop following signs to Brussels and follow the signs to Luik (the Flemish name for Liège). Don't miss this turning or you'll be lost in Brussels Ring Road for an eternity (I'm not kidding!). Skirt around Liège, and pick up signs for E40 Aachen. From here the route is straightforward to Nürburgring – you'll see signs along the way.

Within reason, Nürburgring officials allow every driver to race the course exactly as they wish – slow, fast or insane are all allowed within the obvious strict safety rules (a poster warns every driver to 'Not Be a Hero' on the track. My four thrilling laps achieved a modest time, compared with other drivers around me pushing their cars to the limit (and beyond) – but it honestly didn't diminish the exhilaration. The throaty roar of engine noise was incredible and I got to

Photo: Wolkenkratzer

see the crazy antics of beautiful, powerful cars that passed by in a plume of a dust.

Speed freaks from all over the world fly the flag for their nation at Nürburgring – both on the track and in the stadium. Non-driving friends and family can choose from numerous great viewing spots with unrestricted views across the track – and it doesn't cost a cent to watch. Plenty of food outlets offer traditional German hospitality, including a plate of bratwurst, fried potatoes and sauerkraut washed down with a Bitburger beer. Different days cater for different drives in busy periods, when the grand prix track (called 'VLN') allows an additional full lap at no extra charge. So be sure to check the website.

First-timers are assigned an instructor to guide them around the first lap. A high-performance Lotus is an eye-catching draw, though there is no need for a super-car at Nürburgring – popular models to rent include the Ford Fiesta ST, BMW 3 or 1 series, VW Scirocco and Renault Clio, as well as Japanese sports bikes such as the Suzuki GSXR. Yet almost anyone can race around this breakneck strip of asphalt fresh off the street – in their very own vehicle – for not much more than €20. Nürburgring's speed-freak packages are loaded with added extras, from circuit and stadium tours to autograph sessions. Racing legend Jackie Stewart, on his visit, dubbed the race-track 'Green Hell'. Others insist it is 'Green Heaven'. Either way, it is hard to believe that Nürburgring is a public toll road without a speed limit. However, normal traffic regulations apply – bizarrely – even when adrenaline pushes you to overtake everything and anything in sight. Speed is a strange compulsion behind the wheel. You can feel brave and fearless at first; then a bit shaky with clammy hands and motion sickness. Cramped toes, from brake slamming or leaving a foot hovering above the clutch, can throb in synchronicity with the pulsing of an aching head. An hour-long frown can turn a forehead into Andean-like ridges due to sheer concentration. Propulsion and brake lurches have unsettled my stomach. The yellow flashing lights trackside warn that there's an accident ahead. It's another luxury car with a concertina bonnet. The rush, the roar and the blur of colours can have the feel of a video game. A crash, the smell of burnt rubber and petrol fumes, is a shock reminder that racing on Nürburgring is 100 per cent real. Nasty bends taken badly can mean a heck of a lot of expensive metal. It's kilometre after kilometre of rollicking fun, characterised by steep curves, carousels and rubber-spinning S-shaped bends, blind corners, varying elevations and high octane straits: this circuit can also be one of the most dangerous places on Earth. If the chance of a near-miss or a flip puts you off driving, a pro-driver can be hired to race you around in a specially modified BMW M5 (simply pre-book via Ring Taxi) – a way of encountering the most dangerous curves where so often spin-outs occur in greater safety. Techy petrol heads may also like to know that Nürburgring is a testing centre for major German automobile manufacturers.

This 1927 motor racing track is tricky to master, testing driving skills under demanding conditions that include blind curves, treacherous crests and steep grades. Ever-changing surface conditions and friction require nerve, sensitivity and focus on a route that is free of opposing traffic. A mischievous series of 33 perilous right-hand bends interspersed with 40 bends to the left make this daredevil run a dizzying experience – forget the podium, avoiding a tailspin is the prime goal on this circuit, an amazing feat of showmanship deserving of pole position. Concentration is intense and it's a surprise how soon your nerves, eyes and brakes need a rest. Drives don't start until the morning dew has disappeared – they know better than turn the track into a German tailgate demolition derby event. In a four-hour stint, a trio of cars crashed into the Armco Barriers in a nasty tangle, which serves as a reminder to treat the course with respect. Within seconds, the wreckage is flat-bedded off the track by a truck to the auto-repair shop – I hate to think how big the bill will be. And it's strange to watch a car that passed by earlier crash out in such a state. Instructors warn against complacency once drivers get more comfortable behind the wheel.

My tips? Prepare yourself for a long track with a buzzing atmosphere and bends that are as scary as hell – but fun. Take time to lust over the oh-so-cool exotic cars gleaming in the pit lanes at this iconic auto Shangri-La. You'll share the joys, the ecstasy, the triumphs, the frustrations and untold elation – I've never witnessed so much punching the air or so many man hugs. Yet this isn't just a testosterone frenzy: women, like me, were doing plenty of back-slapping and whoops of pure pleasure. I even indulged in a revved-up victory lap – I swear I have never put my foot down so hard and left it there for so long.

Contacts:
Nürburgring GmbH
www.nuerburgring.de

Nürburgring Information
www.nurburgring.org.uk

PARIS IN A CITROËN 2CV

Culturally, each country has its instantly recognisable design blueprint. Swedes are renowned for sleek, contemporary style; Italians for sexy chic; Germans for smart ingenuity. And the French? Well, just a glance at the Citroën 2CV casts a question mark over France's design panache – a car so ugly that it is now deemed ultra-cute. Dubbed the Ugly Duckling of the Citroën world, the 2CV enjoys a cult following these days: the iconic, slightly gawky, sex symbol of French motor vehicles. Hidden from the Nazis and built for 42 years, the beloved Citroën 2CV has charmed the world for over half a century. It boasts dozens of nicknames across the globe, jernseng (iron bedstead in Norwegian), la cabra (goat in Spanish) and chocolaterias (chocolate tin can in Portuguese) to the rather unkind tin snail (origin unknown). Today, millions of derivatives across 30 different models have been produced across the globe, spawning over 300 2CV automotive clubs and rallies worldwide. Not bad for something its own designer, Pierre Boulanger, admitted looked like an umbrella on wheels.

Citroën unveiled the first 2CV at the prestigious Paris Salon in 1948, yet the original concept was a pre-war 1930s prototype developed in complete secrecy, codenamed TPV (*toute petite voiture*, meaning 'really small car'). Made from lightweight alloys, the early 2CV had a magnesium chassis and wheels. A canvas body stretched over a frame with seats that were merely hammocks suspended from the roof. A set of added-on headlights gave it a nerdy, bug-eyed look, yet French country folk adored the 2CV's go-anywhere suspension. Low earners loved its unbeatable price and even snooty Parisians considered the 600-kilogram (1,323-pound) design revolution beyond fashion. First produced only in grey, other colours followed, representing one of just a few changes to Pierre Boulanger's original design made over the years. Designed to carry four averagely proportioned adults wearing their Sunday-best hats, this space-efficient

Photo: Dolphin674

Photo: Guillaume Speurt

front-wheel-drive boasts a top speed of 60 kilometres (37 miles) an hour. Economical to run, and cheap to maintain, it achieves fuel consumption at three litres per 100 kilometres (0.66 gallons per 62 miles). A three-speed gear box is also equipped with a supercharger peg that acts as a fourth gear. It is capable of running on the worst of roads, can be driven by a debutante and is reassuringly comfy. Even the removable back seats doubled up as a handy picnic bench on a country jaunt over Le Weekend. Yet its proudest boast was that the 2CV was roomy enough for 50 kilograms (110 pounds) of potatoes and yet could transport a basket of eggs over a freshly ploughed field without a single breakage – no mean feat.

Today, the 2CV is cherished by millions for its kooky, romanticly awkward looks and compact, unworldly shape. For a non-streamlined design, it delivers a ride that is incredibly smooth with a well-damped suspension that is couch-like, rather than springy. It is a cosy car: somehow warm, cuddly and forgiving, with more heart than a mere 'old tin car' should rightly possess. The BBC *Top Gear* programme's Jeremy Clarkson may have written the 2CV off as a 'weedy, useless little engine', but the Deux Chevaux (as the French call it, meaning 'two horses') remains the most quintessentially French vehicle to trundle the roads – an automotive that epitomises Gallic charm. Even in Paris, a fleet of 2CVs offers two-person sightseeing trips to tourists (€160 per couple) keen to explore the city in France's cosiest iconic four-wheeled metal cocoon. Somehow the romantic character of the city is heightened by a 2CV journey along old Parisian streets that speak of another era. Available in blue, white and red, the wonderfully cared-for Ugly Ducklings of Paris Authentic offer a rare nostalgic treat around Notre Dame and the tree-lined Champs-Élysées in true French vintage style. Prepare for an automotive treat if you've chosen the much-loved convertible model, as it lends the drive a quintessential laid-back Parisian vibe. Buy one of the more zany travel guidebooks if you have a co-pilot who is happy to relay wacky historical facts, quirky cultural nuggets and out-there political opinions about all the places you pass – it'll heighten the mood on this most idiosyncratic Parisian foray. It's cool to be kooky in the French capital: it'll open doors, help meet the people, know the streets and feel the seasons. For while a BMW, Porsche or Mercedes may be turned away from inaccessible backstreets guarded by stern-chinned security patrols and steel cordons, when the coil-sprung cutesy 2CV rocks up, all comically soft and oddly pliable, it's waved through with a smile. Like an inquisitive fox, the 2CV has a nose for hide-away, secret, not-to-be-missed nooks and corners – so it pays to let the motor roam to sniff these beauties out. While the bodywork shudders, the suspension crashes and rolls, the gearbox rattles and the engine buzzes like a demented bumblebee, the seats of a 2CV soak up most of the lumpiest road-surface bumps of Paris. As you screech around fountain-topped roundabouts in the 2CV's characteristic two-wheel lean of terror, the city's many tourists on foot will gaze at you with true envy – so be certain to stick your beret on as you cruise past L'Opéra, Le Printemps, Moulin Rouge, Sacré-Coeur, St Germain and Les Invalides.

Contacts:
Paris Authentic 2CV Tours
www.parisauthentic.com

ESTORIL COASTAL ROUTE, PORTUGAL

Tracing a delightful route along a striking stretch of Portuguese shoreline, the Costa do Estoril runs from the sandy beach at the wine-making town of Carcavelos – around 15 kilometres (9 miles) from Portugal's historical capital Lisbon – and riddles its way along on the 'marginal' all the way to Guincho to reach the picturesque historic fishing town of Cascais. Though it is often overshadowed by better known and more fashionable parts of the Iberian coastline, this is some of Portugal's most historical terrain: a land rich in architecture built by the Muslim Moors and dazzling legend-steeped beaches. In the late 19th century, King Luis I chose the coast north of Lisbon for his summer residence, sparking renewed interest in the Estoril Coast and its unspoilt, scenic beauty. Pirates laid siege here, mariners set sail from here and noblemen sought glory and praise in its hunting grounds. Today, surfers from around the world arrive here with their boards under their arms, to feast on the rugged Atlantic's great waves, consistent swells and incredible surf culture. With its Mediterranean climate, the Estoril Coastal Route is rightly claiming its place as one of the picturesque shoreline road-trips in Southern Europe – and the natural landscape feels all the more magical with more than 300 days of golden sunshine each year.

The giant double-fronted mansions and pastel-coloured villas along the Estoril Coastal Route provide some tell-tale signs of its affluent past, when royalty holidayed here and built summer houses from which to enjoy curative seaside air. The Atlantic Ocean's clear sparkling waters lap the shores as you motor steadily along the N6 route. For about 33 kilometres (20 miles), driving west from the capital, the

Photo: Wolfgang Pehlemann

ocean melds seamlessly with the sky in a vast expanse of pure, clear cobalt blue.

My first stop was Tamariz Beach (Praia de Tamariz), where I was seduced by an enticing cluster of wide palm-leaf parasols along a neat stretch of perfect sand. I rested my eyes and enjoyed the comfort of the shade to the lullaby sounds of the waves. There's a medieval stone castle here, built to an attractive wedding cake design, but it was locked up tight, so I resolved to wait until Cascais for a stroll. Instead, I watched families picnicking on this generous sandy beach and marvelled at the calm, glassy waters. In summer, at the eastern end of the sands, an ocean-fed swimming pool (Piscina Oceânica do Estoril) attracts crowds of Portuguese schoolchildren while, at the southern end, fishermen line the jetty expectantly with rods and nets.

The road to Cascais arches around in a wide curve, still within sight of the sea and not far from the River Tagus, the longest waterway on the Iberian Peninsula. Flowing westward across Spain, it weaves across Portugal to empty in the Atlantic Ocean on the Estoril Coast. For centuries, the Tagus has irrigated the semiarid lands of rural Portugal along the Estoril Coast and has provided vital water to crops, plants and trees. Fertile waters around Cascais ensure this pretty seaside town is the perfect place to sample some of Portugal's best seafood. Local delicacies include goose barnacle, sweet-tasting shellfish that are harvested from the wild rocky surf by fishermen who risk death to bring them to the region's tables. Briny, plump and with the taste of the sea, goose barnacles are cooked in a groaning copper tub and then served in simple style accompanied by a carafe of inexpensive crisp Portuguese white wine – divine. Cascais, with its swish palatial buildings and old fortress, is a wonderful place to enjoy a stroll in the late afternoon sun.

Praia da Rainha is a small sandy cove just steps from the cobbled streets of the town centre.

Just 12 miles inland, the town of Sintra is a UNESCO World Heritage Site crammed with outstanding castles, gardens and palaces. Surrounded by the pine-covered hills of the Serra de Sintra, the pleasing cooler location of Sintra is what first attracted the nobility and elite of Lisbon to this part of the Portuguese coast. Certainly, the flag-topped, rugged honey-coloured stone of the Moorish castle that overlooks the town is magnificently regal, and dates back to the pre-Christian era when it was built to guard the fertile lands.

Other coastal pit-stops include Praia do Guincho – a large sandy beach and a hotspot for surfers, who always make the most of the east coast waves. Located within the environs of Serra de Sintra National Park, the beach is exposed, untouched and raw. Massive waves, strong swells and the near constant breeze are a major draw for a pro surfing and kiteboarding crowd. In the 1969 James Bond movie *On Her Majesty's Secret Service*, this striking beach was the setting for the pre-title scene, in which 007 (George Lazenby) prevents the suicide of Contessa Vicenzo (Diana Rigg) and fights two men in the sea. Today it appears on sport TV as site of the Portuguese National Surfing and Body Boarding Championships and is a regular on the wind-surfing world championship circuit.

Cabo da Roca – a scenic headland with stunning panoramic views from crumbling cliffs – is known as 'the westernmost point on the European mainland' (as attested by the certificate that visitors to this point can take home with them as a souvenir!). In the 16th century, a fort at Cabo da Roca played an important defensive role in guarding the approach to Lisbon, especially during the Peninsular War. Nowadays all that is left are some mossy remains, together with the lighthouse that still serves as an important warning beacon for shipping. Coastal walks here are beautiful and bracing, along cliff-tops that fall away sharply to the crashing waves of the Atlantic Ocean below.

Contacts:
Portuguese Tourist Board
www.visitportugal.com

COL DE TURINI, FRANCE

As one of the few mountain passes to feature on a top-selling racing video game, the Col de Turini is famous for its helter-skelter corners, blind bends and awkward dog-leg turns, which combined with unpredictable weather makes it is as difficult to conquer as a 3D digital race on a console. An irregular cadence is utterly disarming and no amount of pre-planning this road-trip will get the rainclouds on-side in this part of the Alpes-Maritimes. At 1,607 metres (5,272 feet) above sea level, the Col de Turini has challenged Tour de France riders and car rally drivers alike. Rising steeply up from green-black woodlands, in a series of staggered S-shaped terraced roads neatly trimmed by two-foot grey-slate walls, the road (officially the D 2565) offers incredible sweeping views across the Vésubie valley. From the pretty mountain village of Lantosque, the ascent is a relentless slog up an elongated drag to the summit. While the road itself is a clinical, barren piece of precision engineering with carefully crafted short hairpin turns, the valley is a sprouting tangle of green. It is one heck of a gradient that stretches long and hard for 25 kilometres (15.5 miles), gaining a height of 1,250 metres (4,101 feet) as it spirals up the side of the mountains. Beamed across the world by TV as a famous tight-turn stage of the Monte Carlo Rally, the pass lies near the village of Sospel, between the communes of Moulinet and La Bollène-Vésubie in the arrondissement of Nice.

Over the centuries, both the French and the Italians have squabbled over this Alpine stretch (apparently, Sardinia and Piedmont still feel it is morally theirs). Today, the only battles that take place on the route are fiercely fought motor-sport and cycle challenges – it is used for a full calendar of regional races and international events. It was the highlight of the Tour de France in 1948, 1950 and 1973, though it caused traffic gridlock as far away as Nice. The affluent in-crowds in the plushest resorts of southern France complained and it was decided that the area couldn't cope with being so choked. As the venue for the Monte Carlo Rally, few racing arenas are as spectacular. This is where some of the most skilled drivers in rally history have thrilled assembled motor-sport fans with screeching hairpin turns. But what leaves me utterly agape is that – until fairly recently – the Col de Turini was also driven at night. With only wits, high-beam headlights and a blueprint plan consigned to memory to help navigate the dark. If you're lucky, you'll spot some of the Monaco-based professionals testing their form at the top – a kite-shaped rock serves as the finish line at the end of the hairpin run. The pale, silvery road gets wilder and rougher, patched by stone in places and frayed like cloth around the edges. Pine trees keep stretches of the road damp and dark and it will almost certainly be empty, apart from a cyclist or two, if you drive it mid-week. The crumbling and abandoned stone buildings in the foothills of the mountain look like miniature toys way, way down below. Where the road cuts

Photo: Jérémie Forget

deep into the cliff side, the road has the feel of a fortified castle with rugged ramparts that hug the rocks. A single skinny bridge carries the road for the chapel of Notre Dame de Menour, an obvious landmark on an austere stretch that marks the end of the first climb.

A four-way crossroads marks the summit around which there are some family-run hotels and bars, ski lifts and a large blue sign to mark the top. Keen to go further? Turn right to tag on an extra 17-kilometre loop that ascends sharply for a further 420 metres (1,378 feet) to offer astounding views – few drivers bother, but it is worth it. Pro-cyclists regularly use this stretch for a hill-climb training sprint.

Remember, you're leaving the golden sunshine of the south of France coastal resorts behind – the temperature falls dramatically in the mountains. It takes a lot for this road to close, and it is usually open all year. However, during winter months, it can be blocked after heavy snowfall – so check conditions before you attempt to get to the top. This is not a road to reverse on, do a three-point turn on or break down on – even pro-drivers like Larousse, Thérier, Waldegård, Delecour, McRae, Grönholm and Solberg have been caught out on this narrow, challenging stretch. And the video game? It doesn't have the challenge of driving the route in the same measures as doing it for real. In the digital version, it doesn't really matter if you hit the mountain, or deal a rock a glancing blow, or dump a tank full of fuel all over the track. When the Monte Carlo Rally drivers race the Col de Turini it tests them to their limits, as it has done now for 100 years. As they ascend to the frozen summit and leave the drier sections behind, they gamble their place out on a route that resembles an ice-rink and rely on their wits alone to succeed. No video game, however life-like the graphics, can capture the driving skills required for that.

Contacts:
French Tourist board
www.uk.france.fr

FURKA PASS, SWITZERLAND

The Furka Pass was immortalised by the Aston DB5–Ford Mustang car chase in the legendary James Bond film *Goldfinger* in 1964. The hairpin bends earned their place in cinema history, becoming one of Hollywood's favourite roads, when Tilly Masterson attempted to snipe the villain in front of the Rhône Glacier on the Pass. Today, a driver seeking the full 007 experience can drop by the iconic petrol station – now part of the Aurora Hotel – where Bond and Tilly Masterson go their separate ways when her assassination attempt fails. But you'll probably look anything but Bond-girl glamorous by the time you reach the steps of the Aurora: the steep slopes, blind bends and sharp turns ensuring this drive is a hair-raising trip. Sure, the surface is paved to perfection – this is Switzerland, after all. But this road isn't kind to the foolhardy, the reckless or the meek, and is hostile to those who fail to give it due to respect.

TV shows and motoring message boards describe the Furka Pass as 'utterly terrifying' and it is certainly one of the scariest mountain roads you'll find in the central Swiss Alps. Without safety barriers and guardrails, the route looks precarious and is unbelievably narrow. Every now and again, a concrete post the size of a rolling pin stands between your car and a horrific drop but offers very little comfort – I felt a very genuine need to drive as close to the mountain as I

Photo: Nikater

could manage. It is difficult not to be consumed with visions of the perilous drop and how the smallest steering error could cost you your life on this unpredictable route. On a dry day it is frightening. In poor weather, it adds a whole new dramatic frisson of danger. It rains hard here, ice-cold water pelting the car like bullets that becomes a river that floods the mountain pass. Torrents gush past the car and cascade off the road's sheer edge at an elevation of 2,431 metres (7,976 feet) above sea level. Rainwater can become slush in an instant in Switzerland's snowiest of regions, and it is this magical mix of terror and awe that gives Furka Pass its allure. Today it remains one of the most iconic, exhilarating and nerve-wracking drives on Earth, more than 50 years after 007 swooped round its curves.

Linking the Ursern Valley (Uri canton) with the district of Goms (Valais canton), the Furka Pass ranks as the fourth-highest paved mountain pass in Switzerland. Opened in 1867, and built for strategic military purposes, it was officially Switzerland's longest pass road at the time. Traversing a challenging terrain, the road over the mountains starts with a characteristic pair of tight hairpins just past Gletsch. It then cuts a long sweeping path along the rock-face of the valley, and for around 6 kilometres this super-slick immaculate road makes most drivers beam with pleasure. The smile soon turns to a frown when you switchback on to a steep stretch with a succession of dog-leg turns on a rough track scattered with rock debris. At every blind corner, it's impossible not to hold your breath as you wonder what lies in wait: will it be blocked by fresh snowfall, cloaked in heavy mist or will there be an oncoming vehicle? Poor visibility is part of the character of this drive and you're certain to spend some time in heavy clouds. Avalanches, icy patches, blizzards and landslides can occur anytime. Should the weather not waylay you, then the views definitely will: be sure to leave plenty of time to travel this road – this really isn't a route to rush and miss out on all the incredible views. Regular look-out points are well-used by the quarter-million people that journey the pass each year – testament that it takes more than sheer drops, gut-wrenching hairpin bends, precipitous slopes and serpentine twists and turns to put road-trippers off. Once the most dangerous and difficult stretches are behind you, the rest of the Furka Pass is a smoother ride – though not after dark or when it showers. Towards the end of the loop, it rolls through numerous scenic valleys that are home to pretty Swiss villages. The final ascent requires a pedal to the metal to roar to the top of the Furka Pass along a road punctured with moon-like craters. From Amsteg, the climb is a long 42 kilometres (26 miles) with an elevation gain of 1,942 metres (6,371 feet). Your reward for reaching the top without mechanical failure or mishap? Some breathtaking views across a small lake hemmed in by flowering alpine scrub, bathed in a milky silver light.

Drivers with plenty of derring-do will breeze along the descent. Others will cling cautiously to the side of the mountain. Be warned: the road picks up pace on a steep string of spiral turns. The road also tapers to little more than an asphalt ribbon for a straight drag at the end.

The very best bit? Well as being one of the 'Big 3' interconnected passes close to Andermatt, the road wriggles within a few hundred metres of the Rhône Glacier, source of the River Rhône. Although the glacier has retreated dramatically in recent years, it is still vast. Sweaty-palmed drivers who have survived the pass intact can park up and stretch their jelly legs inside the glacier itself: a crazy adventure on a crazy route.

Contacts:
Switzerland Tourist Board
www.myswitzerland.com

STELVIO PASS, ITALY

If a movie were made of the Stelvio Pass it would have a million thrilling twists and turns and a dramatic finish, for this mountain cut-through in Stelvio National Park in Italy's South Tyrol is mainly hairpin bends. It may not possess great beauty, but it boasts eye-catching theatre as the second-highest pass in the Alps at 2,757 metres (9,045 feet) by just 12 metres. Voted 'Best Driving Road in the World' by TV car show *Top Gear* in 2008 for its wall of 48 switchback turns running up its north face, travelling this ultra-high route is guaranteed to make any set of brakes smoke. The descent is like going to hell in a handcart: it's one heck of a driving experience, but one that may just make your head explode.

Built between 1820 and 1825 by the Austro-Hungarian Empire for military purposes to link the region of Lombardia with the rest of Austria, the road was designed by Carlo Donegani. Today it is much as it was then and is considered a masterpiece of civil engineering. By the end of the First World War, the Stelvio Pass formed the border between the Austro-Hungarian Empire, Switzerland and Italy, but had lost its strategic military importance. The SS38, as it is officially known, became little more than a local route. Until, that is, *Top Gear* blew a mighty great fanfare and raised its profile world-wide.

To get the most out of the drive, be sure to hit the road nice and early. You can reach Bormio from Milan via Lecco in under three hours – then it's up along the SS38 for 32 mad kilometres (20 miles). Motorbike nuts love this road too and form fearless kamikaze swarms to tackle the ascent en masse. They don't arrive until lunchtime or later. The majority of skid marks that etch the road are from speeding bikes. If you can, choose a mid-week day and avoid the peak holiday months of July and August, otherwise you may well be nose-to-bumper. *Top Gear*'s bold claims have seen traffic volume on this route more than treble – and this is one place you really don't want a prang.

Driving from the north-west side is the only logical direction to approach the route, in my opinion. From this direction, departing from Prato, you'll get the buzz from the steep ascent and the non-stop run of blind hairpins. Do it from the other direction and it'll feel like you're dropping a stone. The ascent side also ensures you get a decent run through the heart of the Stelvio National Park before the climb starts: this sleek, fast road slices through thick alpine forests. From the foot of the pass, the switchbacks come fast and furious. Each is numbered (look for the stone markers by the side of the road), so if you're feeling dizzy you can see how far it is until you reach the top. Half-way it gets progressively harder as the switchbacks start to show their teeth. One or two blind bends are fine, but after a dozen your forehead starts to crease. Every tight turn threatens to send you off the edge. Each pothole seems determined to make you disappear. Every twist presents a technical driving challenge. You daren't blink. The concentration swells your eyeballs. There's no way you're prepared to loosen your grip on the steering wheel, even though beads of sweat are forming on your brow. And for the millionth time you question the sanity of thinking this might be fun.

The last stretch up towards the top of the pass is a

Photo: Zairon

rougher section of road. Snow can settle here and it can be icy too. And there's an ever-present risk of oncoming traffic. Bits of paving have crumbled. Hitting the summit is a relief, and a triumph – you can't help but raise your face towards the heavens to give thanks. OK, Stelvio Pass doesn't offer incredible variety or a nice journey flow, but it is still something special. I breathed in the mountain air from a bench by a food joint. Both my stomach and head felt like they were still in motion. The views at 2,750 metres are lovely but the smells of onions, sauerkraut and bratwurst were a serious test. I grabbed a jacket – there's a biting wind – until the nausea cleared.

As I gazed out over the bleak rocky slopes, I recalled passing a memorial to the fallen First World War soldiers. It was set on the roadside on a particularly desolate and exposed stretch without trees under which to shelter or hide. I shivered; as a place of bloody combat it would have felt a million miles from home and a lonely, vulnerable place in which to lose your life. Stelvio Pass is described in Italian military history as the place where 'the world's highest battle was fought'; bodies of fallen soldiers, mummified by the cold, have been uncovered in recent thaws.

Leaving the summit to drive down the other side of the Stelvio Pass feels a bit like falling off a mountain. There's an urge to shut your eyes and hold on for dear life as the scenery rushes by in fast-forward. At the bottom of the descent, you're spat out unceremoniously in Bormio. By this time, the brakes are red-hot, you've got a banging head, your pulse is racing – but it enters your mind to do it all again.

Contacts:
Italian Tourist Board
www.italiantouristboard.co.uk

ALSACE ROUTE DES VINS, FRANCE

The scenery may be postcard picturesque but don't let the genteel charm of the Route des Vins deceive you: discovering Alsace requires a robust engine to master epic uphill slogs on this long and 'wine-ding' road. On some of the steepest ascents, it may feel wise to ditch the car as even the slowest of insects seems to pass you by. Whining protestations from a gear box mid-climb can wobble the steadiest nerves. Alien wheezes, mechanical wails and haunting howls can all be emitted from the sturdiest of engines when they are under hill-climb pressure. In an open top Mini Cooper, the searing summer heat on the route's shadeless climbs is a gruelling test of endurance for passengers and driver. Thankfully, a scattering of rustic stone water-fountains break up the journey with frequent much-needed irrigation. On long, sloping descents, a Mini Cooper can fly like the wind as if it were a go-cart free-wheeling downhill at speed. With tangled hair, and windswept cheeks, the views are not just of France but of Germany and the Rhine. What's more you're passing 119 wine-growing half-timbered villages in a rainbow of bubble-gum hues.

Road-trippers in the Alsace region often begin their journey in Strasbourg, where traffic-heavy streets and congested suburbs should be navigated early to avoid tedious delays. Pick up the road out to the north-west and head to the prettiest stone villages around Blienschwiller, less than 40 kilometres (25 miles) away. Stretching some 170 kilometres (106 miles), the entire Wine Route from Gimbrett in the north to Leimbach in the south is doable in a long weekend. The vivid hues that this region is famous for are bold, intense and seductive: from the blue-green Vosges Mountains and the dark crags of the Black Forest to the olive-green terraces of around 14,500 hectares (35,830 acres) of tufted vines and gorgeous multi-coloured villages, the Route des Vins is like a brightly daubed paintbox – almost all of it traffic-free.

More than 8 million visitors make the pilgrimage to the Wine Route each year, arriving from all over continental Europe and the UK. Exploring the vineyard trails and roadside stalls in some of France's most stunning countryside soon distracts even the most diligent driver from the hills – though challenges to conquer lurk behind every brow. Though a map can warn of upcoming hills, the spaghetti riddle of wiggly lines on paper doesn't always do an engine-screeching chug justice. On a relatively flat stretch of winding road through Dambach-la-Ville, Dieffenthal, Scherwiller, Kintzheim and Châtenois, all thoughts of hills faded as our Mini Cooper eased itself smoothly around curvaceous bends. It was, however, merely a light appetiser for a meatier entrée: an endless incline through yellow-green vines on a landscape dotted with Gothic spires and turrets out to an imposing plateau topped by forest, ramparts and ancient ruins. Meadows of sweet-smelling wildflowers softened the blow that there was another such gruelling climb ahead. After a downhill rush of rural scenery, during which our adrenaline surged as we watched the speedometer hit the max, the route widened and levelled. The Mini Cooper enjoyed a moment of heady freedom on a vine-hemmed open road before an epic skyward climb loomed oh-so-large on the approach to the hamlet of Rorschwihr. Each passenger, like me, pressed an accelerator foot hard into the floor in the hope it would somehow give the engine extra oomph. We lowered our heads and gritted our teeth, as if in solidarity with 1,140 kilograms (2,513 pounds) of shiny cherry-red metal, and willed it steadily up towards the top.

As the Mini Cooper pounded the road slowly with gutsy determination, it felt like Alsace's rows of proud vines were standing in unified salute as it inched its way forward. When, at last, the engine edged triumphantly to the summit, a field of beaming, weathered farm-workers stood and cheered. We rested for a while, and patted the Mini Cooper with pride, as an elderly farm truck clattered by at a snail's pace, billowing silver-grey smoke. Agricultural methods in some of the magnificent Wine Route's Gallic-Germanic farm villages have barely altered in centuries and much of the labour on its vine-clad contours is still with hand tools and scythes. A flock of super-fit professional road-racing cyclists whooshed effortlessly by, legs waxed and oiled. It made us restless; competitive even. So we set off in the wake of these über humans: the Mini Cooper roared loudly as if triggered by an incredible power surge. The cyclists, now out-of-the-saddle in a sprint in pursuit of something distant, were now a moving cloud of dust on the horizon.

The barrel-fronted Gilbert Dontenville winery signifies that Ribeauvillé is just a few kilometres away, along an immaculate tarmac carpet. Slithers of scrumptious *tarte flambé* are served at the roadside here and after looping a couple of mini-roundabouts we were on the road to Riquewihr. Once again, the route is distinctly bucolic with a light scattering of simple farm buildings on rounded yellow meadows. The long climb to Hunawihr and Riquewihr weaves past the bougainvillea-filled barrels where the pastel-coloured buildings with jutting Rapunzel-like towers and Cinderella spires ensure a magical end to this section of the Wine Route. For the perfect finale, seek out a crisp sparking Crémant at the Au Cep de Vigne (well, we are on the Route des Vins…) and toast the plucky Mini Cooper to the energetic strains of Bavarian oompah classics.

Photo: Maximilian Dörrbecker (Chumwa)

Contacts:
Régional du Tourisme d'Alsace
www.tourisme-alsace.com

Alsace Route des Vins
www.alsace-route-des-vins.com

THE GREAT DOLOMITE ROAD, ITALY

In Italian it is the Strada dell Dolomiti, but English-speakers know it as the Great Dolomite Road: a route that runs from the eastern edge of the town of Bolzano right through the mountains to beautiful Cortina d'Ampezzo. The unadulterated, unelaborated trip snakes across an all-important arterial through towering peaks for about 140 kilometres (86 miles) along the SS241 (Bolzano to Val di Fassa) and SS48 (Val di Fassa to Cortina d'Ampezzo). In winter, glass-like icy roads offer a treacherous trip through the snow-capped Dolomites. Some adventurous souls, their cars equipped with spiked tyres and high-beam lights, slide around hair-raising hairpin bends and down steep slopes, within a few feet of snow drifts. Ice-climbers rave about the challenging overhangs and tough ice-clad ascents, but I'm more than content navigating the Dolomite peaks in my car. Even the simplest climbs require axes, crampons, helmets, mountaineering boots, thermal clothing and ice protection – not to mention brute strength, agility and stamina. From what I've seen when I've driven this route, it also helps to be a little bit crazy. It takes a certain type of madness to climb 1,000-foot-high ice-covered verticals without handholds brandishing an ice pick. Little wonder they breathe deeply, and avoid looking down.

I do, however, carry in my car boot: head lamps, karabiners, ski poles, goggles, fleece hat, mountain mitts, a thermal coverall and a basic expedition kit, some first aid items and an ice axe. My greatest fears are avalanches, rock and ice falls or mechanical failure miles from anywhere, so I always plan ahead before setting off to drive the Great Dolomite Road. Though stretches of the road have been modernised, very little in the area has altered in centuries. Though it is possible to drive the whole route in four hours, the stars would need to align in perfect synchronicity for you to do so. The briefest shower will slow you down. Dismal skies cast hindering shadows. Low cloud can make conditions challenging. Don't even think of attempting it in a serious downpour.

The construction of the Great Dolomite Road began in the 19th century and took decades to complete: it was a complex route that formed a formidable obstacle in northern Italy. For centuries, travelling through the Alps was nearly impossible. Now a good full day is all it takes to do a journey in a car that once took many, many days to do on foot. The ski resort town of Bolzano in South Tyrol denotes the start of the Strada dell Dolomiti and is a town with a pleasing fusion of Germanic and Italian cultures. Every region in Italy has dialects, but in the Dolomites they are much more noticeable. For a start, road signs allow for local dialects (the most famous being Ladino or Ladin, spoken near Bolzano) and, additionally, they are in Italian and German too. Food also mixes German into the Italian food traditions, with hearty mountain food rich in salami, seeded breads, strong alcohol, mushrooms, tomatoes and a zillion different types of cheese. Ladin cuisine is a big part of the local culture, with typical dishes such as 'Crafuncins' (stuffed pasta) or

Photo: Lunardo0

'Puessl' (apple pancake, cut into small pieces) made using traditional recipes passed on through the generations. The traditional dress – laced bodice and petticoat skirt, nipped in at the waist for women and mountain britches and peasant hat for men – is very Germanic in style. Yet the identity is distinct and fiercely Ladin, and unique.

Running east to west, to Cortina d'Ampezzo, on a string of skinny mountain roads, the route reaches out from the steep canyons of the Eggental Gorge to the greener-than-green Lake Karersee, a spring-fed body of water fringed with bird-filled vegetation that was much-beloved by the Austrian Empress Elisabeth. Keep hands clamped tightly on the wheel as you scour the route ahead for rising peaks of the Vajolet Towers on the way to the pretty village of Vigo di Fassa. Though the road wiggles like unfurled ribbon, the Rosengarten Mountain Range stands rigid and proud in the background as another series of terrifying turns approaches at the mid-way point at Canazei. Legs need a stretch? Then follow the road to Malga Ciapela for a relaxing cable-car ride up to giant peaks at 3,254 metres (10,676 feet), where you'll be utterly wowed by incredible views.

From Canazei, select a low gear for the steep ascent and brutal twists up to Passo Pordoi in Veneto – at the top take time to breathe in the sweeping panorama across the snow-dusted ranges of the Marmolada, Rosengarten and Sassolungo mountains. Shift gears for the rapid descent on the road to Arabba – one of the most celebrated mountain passes with hard-core road-trippers because of its 80+ hairpin bends. From the narrow stretch across the Passo di Falzarego, the road weaves through an ancient pine-clad valley before shooting through a couple of dark, cold tunnels and emerging into bright Italian sunlight at Cortina d'Ampezzo. Known as simply 'Cortina' by the locals, this sophisticated ski resort is beloved by the Italian glitteratti with its top-notch alpine skiing, mountaineering and Nordic ski scene and a calendar packed with swanky international ski *soirées*. Non-skiers will relish the swish boutiques, gourmet cafes and upscale watering holes that cater for the A-list crowd in slow mode. Congratulations – you've completed one of the most scenic roads in Europe! Time for a glass of chilled Italian wine to toast the Great Dolomite Road with its resplendent gorges, gushing streams and dramatic rocky peaks.

ROUTE NAPOLÉON, SOUTH-WEST FRANCE

There is something about the pace of the Route Napoléon that causes me to drum my fingers against the steering wheel as if I am pounding along to the beat of a military marching band. Martial manoeuvres have long been accompanied by music and as I am driving the route taken by France's most famous leader in history, I can't help but beat my 'drum'. I imagine the soldiers, under Napoléon's command, regulated by a percussive rhythm. The troops are stepping in perfect time with murderous thought for their opponents. They are synchronised, energised and pounding the rocky path as one. Napoléon Bonaparte marched this route, after escaping house arrest in Elba, to Grenoble in 1815 to overthrow Louis XVIII. With his 1,000 men he marched the route I'm now journeying by car: an undulating 325-kilometre stretch of the N85 that begins at Golfe-Juan in the French Riviera and extends all the way to the southern pre-Alps, where it weaves through the spectacular mountains of Provence.

For the Route Napoléon, I have hired a sporty little Renault as it is a smooth road, I'm told, with few challenges. Cambered corners and fantastic scenery combine to ensure easy journeying. I'm assured that wide, sweeping roads offer long stretches with high numbers that you can speed through – should you want to. The car's Energy TCe 130 engine enjoys an easy, fast road and I'm keen to test out the performance of this motor: I'm told this new Megane model offers loads more toque. Without a zippy Sports Tourer, it took Napoléon and his troops a whole week to navigate the route, but I'm planning to drive it in a day. I've got an audio version of the Bonaparte story ready to play on the car stereo, as seems fitting as I ride through rousing scenery. It's good to mull over Napoléon while keeping half an eye on the distinctive road signs with their brown eagle motif that promise to keep me on-track.

The road was inaugurated in 1932 and runs through Provence from Golfe-Juan, before turning to the A-list resort of Cannes in the swanky French Riviera. Napoléon and his men apparently rested on the beach at Cannes briefly. I decided to do the same, after paying almost €10 for a coffee (ouch!), and spent much of the next half-hour gawping at monied beach-goers of pensionable age wearing G-string beachwear – both genders. In 1815 I'm pretty certain that Napoléon didn't have to suffer that. I then headed to the perfume-making town of Grasse with its pretty courtyards and echoing backstreets. Heading south-west, the route passes Saint-Vallier-de-Thiey, where I feel I could linger for a while to enjoy a picnic lunch Napoléon-style. He ate here with his men; as a military leader he was fastidious, concerning himself with the minutiae of his troops' diet, right down to the individual ingredients in the soup.

What made Bonaparte so detail-orientated? Well, he was born on the Mediterranean island of Corsica to a local family in 1769, shortly after it had come under French jurisdiction. The island's distinctive culture of close-knit ties and community shaped Napoléon's nature and values. Aged eight, the young Bonaparte was sent to school in France on a scholarship for the sons of impoverished noble families. His Corsican accent and poor grasp of French made him a target for teasing (in later life he would insist that he considered himself French rather than Corsican). Napoléon was an intelligent and determined student and a career in the artillery via the royal military school in Paris beckoned. In 1785, he entered an artillery regiment and thrived on the mental and physical challenges of war. His resilience was astounding: he could survive on little sleep, go for weeks without changing his shirt and was fanatical about planning in order to leave nothing to chance. Yet arguably this greatest skill – and one that served him well on the Napoléon Route, was his ability to generate great loyalty from his men. Food is all-important to a soldier, far from home. And this, I imagine, is why he made it his business to nourish them well.

As a lunch venue, St Vallier is magical: set on a high plateau of lush green and overlooked by soaring hills, St Vallier began as a Roman stronghold, and contains a Romanesque church dating back to the early 12th century. I imagine Bonaparte losing himself to his thoughts in the valley's hypnotic views. Next, the road heads towards Castellane and this is where the road undergoes a change of pace: the fast-flowing route starts to curl up like a ribbon after marching along, for hours, like a Napoleonic army. Actually, it's a shock as a driver to be suddenly faced with a succession of 180-degree turns after a lazy morning's cruising. But, after a shift in gears, I reacquaint myself with the brakes and enjoy the new-found thrills of the route. From the appreciative purr from

Photo: Sébastien Thébault

the Renault's engine, it seems to be enjoying being tested in a whole new way.

Napoléon himself was tested, during the Hundred Days – the short-lived period of his reign after his escape from Elba before his defeat at Waterloo. Yet he was forward-thinking enough to plan ahead and secure the future of the Napoleonic legend by dictating his memoirs in this battle-charged period. My audio history – fascinating so far – labours the point that Napoléon relished the prospect of glory above all else on several occasions. He was a vain man, apparently: proud that his yellowish pallor showed off his particularly fine white teeth. At 5 feet 6 inches he wasn't statuesque, but his troops adored him, inspired by his driving force and dangerous ambition.

I pass the handsome Napoléon Bridge close to where his men were fed – again. Along from here is Château de Brondet, where the mayor famously insisted Napoléon stay the night. Then it's a steep slog over beautiful Col des Lèques at 1,146 metres (3,759 feet) – a popular mission with slick flocks of road-race cyclists. The road passes through Clue de Taulanne and the small village of Barrême, before it reaches Digne-les-Bains. Turning slightly westward, following the Bléone river until Malijai, the road resumes its journey south-westward to Sisteron. When Napoléon arrived at this well-ordered town, he was braced for local resistance but he was allowed to stay unchallenged. In fact, he ordered his men to take a break and rest – I was tempted to do the same, when I spotted a museum that, curiously, is dedicated to the Baden-Powell Scout Movement. It was closed (as are most museums in France on a Monday), so I pushed on up to cross over the Col Bayard (1,248 metres/4,094 feet) to the pretty village of Corps. Further north is La Mure, another flower-filled town set around a fountain. The route then leads all the way to Grenoble – its final destination and the end of a remarkable drive. Not only has it been a truly thrilling driving experience, but it has felt like I've followed Napoléon's marching boots in a moving and meaningful way. I've learned a lot about the man and enjoyed some rewarding moments in the places he also did, by beautiful gorges, canyons and mountain villages. 'A leader is a dealer in hope', Napoléon once uttered. Me, I hope I have a chance to drive along the Route Napoléon in his footsteps again.

THE ALPENSTRASSE, GERMANY

There's a nice, percussive rhythm to driving the 450-kilometre (280-mile) route from Lindau on Lake Constance to Schönau on Lake Königssee that instinctively makes me tap my fingers on the wheel. Curvaceous roads roll seductively: there are few exceptions and no extremes, just rounded swells. From lush Bavarian meadows and soft, velvety hills to thick green woods, romantic valleys and glistening lakes: the Alpenstraße rolls effortless through them all. All around, the sounds of the Bavarian Alps add the rousing symphony of Mother Nature: a concerto of melodic birdsong that echoes across the region's picturesque wooded valleys. Little wonder that the Alpine Road is Germany's oldest touring road.

First mentioned in 1879 as part of a published historical travelogue from 1858 by the Bavarian King Maximilian II (1811–1864), the German Alpenstraße is still, in many respects, the very same route it was then. In the late 1920s the nation's chief medical officer proposed the development of a proper road on health wellness grounds, insisting that

Photo: Karl Gruber

the travelling public simply deserved to experience the outstanding beauty of the transition of the Bavarian Alps, from Lindau to Berchtesgaden – a thoroughly modern justification for that age. In 1932, the argument gained clout when the German Touring Club drew up infrastructure plans for the route's creation. It would be a costly project requiring a significant amount of construction, but one that would benefit the health of the nation, it was decided.

Ground was broken in 1933 with approximately 274 kilometres (170 miles) of road completed within the first six years. War, social unrest and other interruptions delayed the route's progress for more than 25 years. As one of Hitler's prestige projects, it involved expanding existing trails and creating some routes from scratch. However, in 1960 it was finally completed, attracting visitors from near and far for the pure driving pleasure of a smooth road between two of Germany's most stunning lakes. It remains one of the country's most-loved stretches, with its breathtaking views and uniquely rich Bavarian culture, such as colourful country weddings, age-old local fairs and old-style German zither and brass band music.

A world-famous aspect of Bavarian culture is its musicians, glugging Pilsner from steins while wearing the traditional knee-length leather britches (*Lederhosen*) at the region's Oktoberfest events. Though centuries have passed since farm-working peasants wore the lederhosen while cultivating the lower slopes of the Bavarian Alps, you may catch a glimpse of the outfit in some of the old-style eateries strung along the German Alpine Road. Tucked in among cattle fields scattered with herds responsible for the delicious mountain cheeses that are sold from roadside stalls along the route, these Alpine inns with beer gardens have served road-trippers journeying the Bavarian landscape for umpteen generations.

As well as scenery and sustenance, the Alpenstraße is also dotted with at least 100 spas offering a wide range of different wellness and beauty treatments. Germanic spas are well-known for their spartan health regimes and though many now are decadent and luxurious, a certain rigour and austerity is still maintained. Health by deprivation? Far from it. I soaked it up and felt amazing – and not just the mineral-rich natural spring waters with their curative, healing powers. The region's fresh local produce and steam-cloaked bath-houses combine to truly invigorate the body. Once you've stripped off – as in most of Germany's wellness resorts, bare flesh and good health go hand-in-hand here with clothing surplus to requirements – it's time to chill out and relax and sample the Alpenstraße's other great liquid: frothy-topped Pilsner beer.

Many drivers choose to start at the official beginning of the route in Lindau, a genteel historic town overlooking a gorgeous harbour. Follow the route out of town with its seven curves, where the Rohrbach stream rises through Lindenberg – dubbed 'Little Paris' in the early 20th century on account of its hat-making tradition that once saw around 8 million straw hats made there each year. Out through the edge of the Nagelfluhkette National Park, with views out to the distant Swiss Säntis Massif, the journey is almost a drive-in movie experience with epic full-screen views of technicolour valleys, hills and meadows. At Oberstaufen, the region's capital of wellness, the B308 road meanders through lush, green forests with the 1,300-metre (4,265-foot) peaks of the Voralpenland (Alpine Upland) as a spectacular backdrop. At Nesselwang, pull over at a parking spot just before the entrance to town for a beautiful spot for a selfie or to take a commemorative snap of the authentic little German ginger-bread mountain town surrounded by towering alpine peaks.

Follow the B309, and then take the B310 to Füssen, where the route joins the fairy-tale castles and pretty fields of the famous Romantic Road (B16). Cross over the River Lech to visit the custard-coloured spire-topped neo-Gothic Schloss Hohenschwangau, built in the 19th century by Maximilian II of Bavaria. His successor, Ludwig II, later lived there, building a bigger, more ostentatious castle in 1868 and where he drowned in suspicious circumstances after just a few months.

Pass through pretty villages that lead to winter ski resorts that in summer fill with brightly coloured wild flowers. Drive on to the mountain town of Wallgau, where pretty red-roofed Alpine chalets cling to flower-filled slopes. Nearby, a handsome dome-topped monastery makes the very most of the area's peaceful tranquillity – the only interruption to the monastic silence is the sound of birdsong.

At the small town of Bad Tölz, a historic healing centre of medieval character on the western bank of the Isar River, the route winds through the Chiemgau Alps. Rising up to an elevation of 1,800 metres (5,905 feet), this German hotspot for winter sports, mountain biking, trekking, trout fishing and golf signifies the approach road to beautiful Berchtesgaden – look out for a roadside sprinkling of snow, even during springtime. Germany's second-tallest mountain, the Watzmann, is here, famous as the favourite holiday destination of Hitler during the Second World War. You can even enjoy afternoon tea in the Kehlsteinhaus (also known as the Eagle's Nest) – a 50th birthday present to Hitler from the Nazi movement that sits in mountains above Berchtesgaden. Today the building is owned by a charitable trust and has indoor tables and an outdoor beer garden; you can't access it by car and it'll take two hours to hike it on foot, though there is a bus that passes by from Obersalzberg and rattles up the mountain: a bump-and-bruise adventure that boasts awesome views and makes a notable way to end a Bavarian trip.

Contacts:
Touristikverein Deutsche Alpenstraße
www.deutsche-alpenstrasse.de

D-DAY BEACHES, NORMANDY, FRANCE

The Normandy Coast of northern France conjures up images of cheese-making villages and apple orchards surrounded by lush green fields scattered with brown-and-white dairy cattle. Yet this charming region of France and its rugged beach-hemmed landscape has a deeper poignancy as the site of the D-Day landings. On 6 June 1944 around 150,000 British, Commonwealth and American troops came ashore at dawn to liberate France from Nazi forces. It was to be a fateful mission. Unknown to the brave young soldiers, a torrent of German gunfire from high above the landing beaches awaited them as they waded ashore. It was a horrific onslaught and the Allied troops took heavy casualties. However, it was a daring, bold and important military operation that marked the beginning of the end of the Second World War.

The scene is so peaceful now, the horrors of over 70 years ago seem almost impossible. Yet massive parts of Hitler's coastal defences, known as the Atlantic Wall, remain to this day. Also along the coast, you'll find luxury marine spas, seafood restaurants and family-orientated shoreline resorts as well as the memorials and war museums dedicated to the many lives lost. Yet it is the sight of the neat military cemeteries with thousands of white headstones that brings home the scale of the D-Day landings. As immortalised so compellingly in the Steven Spielberg film *Saving Private Ryan*, so many men made the ultimate sacrifice in the largest seaborne invasion in world history.

Normandy's beaches, from the bird-filled Carentan estuary to the little port town of Ouistreham, were divided into five strategic points by the Allies. Each has its own character and codename: Utah, Omaha, Gold, Juno and Sword. Look carefully: you can still spot the German bunkers, gun batteries and other evidence of the intense fighting that took place. It is a rewarding place to walk and think: there's a lot to see and mull over. The wide, airy beaches under big skies are beautiful and inspiring rather than bleakly depressing. Children play in rock pools, families gather mussels and couples stroll the sands holding hands.

Exploring the coast by road isn't at all difficult: all the D-Day attractions are well-signed (in a variety of languages) as a result of the 70th memorial year in 2014. Most visitors see the landing beaches on a 250-kilometre (155-mile) round trip from Ouistreham to Caen, riding along the coast in one direction and inland in the other. Some may prefer a one-way trip between the ferry port of Cherbourg and Ouistreham–Caen; regular cross-channel ferries from Portsmouth in South England serve this route.

Stretches of the rippling Normandy coastal road skirt the shore for miles and miles. Steeper sections surround both Omaha and Gold beaches, but every section is paved and well-maintained apart from a few roughshod loose-stone tracks that run down to the sea over dunes. It is easy to park up and walk along the same rock-trimmed sandy shores where the Allied troops landed and braved a hail of enemy fire. As I strolled the sands, I passed elderly men walking with their grandchildren on their way to pay their respects.

Utah Beach is a long rod-straight stretch of undeveloped coast, 20 kilometres (12 miles) from Omaha by sea (it's more than double this by land via Carentan). A fine Navy memorial stands proudly at one end of the beach together with a small D-Day museum. A landing craft beside the museum vividly conveys what the troops had to endure. To weaken German defences, Allied paratroops were dropped in during the night. In the pitch black one unlucky soldier landed on top of the village church at Ste-Mère-Eglise. His parachute got tangled in the tower and he was discovered suspended in full view of the Germans at first light. Today a dummy parachutist hangs from the church roof, the strangest of all the D-Day memorials.

Omaha Beach is reached by a roller-coaster route that passes a walking path to the huge cliff-top Longues-sur-Mer German gun emplacement where weapons are still in place. As the landing spot for more than 40,000 American troops, the beach is the scene of the greatest loss of American life in the D-Day operation. A barrage of German mortars, machine guns and artillery had a devastating effect on the invasion – thousands were killed on the sand (depicted in the shocking and bloody opening scenes of Steven Spielberg's war epic *Saving Private Ryan*, which won praise for its historical accuracy). Craters left by falling shells still scar this otherwise idyllic coastline and there is a fine museum that showcases the D-Day landings and details the human side of the conflict. The Normandy American Cemetery & Memorial has regular informative tours around the cemetery that give you some of the stories behind the graves.

Stretching between Le Hamel and Ver-sur-Mer, Gold Beach was the scene of some of the fiercest British beach fighting, with the invading troops facing heavy German resistance. Sea defences and even a gun emplacement can

Photo: dynamosquito

still be explored by visitors to Ver-sur-Mer and a simple memorial plaque stands at the top of the beach paying respect to those who fought there. It was here that Company Sergeant Major Stanley Hollis earned the only Victoria Cross of the D-Day landings after single-handedly storming two enemy pill-boxes and later saving two of his comrades who had been pinned down by enemy fire.

Juno Beach was invaded by units of the Canadian 3rd Infantry Division, who took heavy casualties in the first wave but eventually managed to wrest control of the area from defending German troops. The Canadians had more than just the Germans as obstacles to contend with: the natural offshore reefs presented a dangerous underwater hazard that delayed the assault for an hour to allow the landing craft to clear the reef on the rising tide. The German 716th Infantry Division, particularly the 736th Regiment, provided excellent defence of the area from strong firing positions. As the Canadians waded ashore, there was little fire at first, mainly because the German gun pits and giant concrete casements were set to ensure the line of fire pointed just beyond the beach in order to prevent an enemy onslaught from the sea. The first wave – Company B of the Royal Winnipeg Rifles – took dreadful casualties and was reduced to 1 officer and 25 men as it moved towards the seawall. By evening the Canadians had suffered 1,200 casualties.

Sword Beach is the furthest east of the codenamed landing beaches, an 8-kilometre stretch of coast from Ouistreham to Saint-Aubin-sur-Mer. Set beside the Orne River estuary, British troops landed here and fought their way towards the nearby bridge over the river. A thrilling and decisive course of action had taken place during the previous night, when airborne troops, using gliders, landed right beside the bridge and captured it.

Contacts:
Normandy Info
www.normandy-france.net

GARDEN ISLAND, DENMARK

Even an enchanting land of fairy-tale make-believe has its monsters, but in the land of Hans Christian Andersen the demons are a composition of nature. For among the magical fields of flowers, castles and windmills that provided inspiration for the storyteller's tales of fairies and princesses are some fiendish roads. Not dangerous. Not potholed. Just unspeakably slow. Criss-crossing manicured asphalt roads, these rugged tyre-worn trails cut through the hop-filled meadows of the South Fyn archipelago through landscape that has spawned pages of story-book narrative. To journey this region by car is to power through a legend-steeped chapter of mysterious dark woodlands, moat-ringed towers and spiked spires. Marking the centre of Denmark, this circular 'Garden Island' forms a convenient 2,985-square-kilometre (1,153-square-mile) stepping-stone that picturesquely bridges the coastal channel between Jutland and Zealand.

As befitting an outdoorsy nation, the roads of Denmark are full of keen cyclists with over 100 of the country's several hundred cycle routes running through the Funen region. Add to this a steady flotilla of rattling farm vehicles – tractors, carts, crop-spraying trucks and hop wagons, to name just a few – and it's easy to establish why patience is a virtue on Funen's slow-moving roads. Overtaking is impossible (and road-rage futile in a region so serene and laid-back), so motorists soon learn to settle back in their seats, better

Photo: Peter Larsen

acquaint themselves with third gear and revel in the region's pastoral delights.

A particularly scenic route connects the tiny market town of Bogense with Odense via the glorious sweeping blonde-sand beaches of Hasmark Strand. Sitting on the north coast of the Garden Island, Hasmark Strand looks out across the Baltic coastline with rolling green hills behind it. Small clusters of half-timbered houses make up the old-fashioned fishing villages that are still home to sea-legged mariners poised for combat with sand eel, herring and cod. Richly nourished by a maritime climate that is the trademark of Denmark's second-largest island, Funen is blessed with dark soils, fertile pasture and bleached stone that declare it's wet in winter, dry in summer and sea-sprayed in between.

Funen's gently undulating countryside makes for pleasant driving as only a couple of intimidating hills slow vehicular progress down to below a walking pace. When cyclists weave onto off-road trails, the open road allows for a burst of automotive exhilaration – however brief. Like the Danes, it is customary to pull over into hidden back-roads for near-hourly snacks of herring, rye bread and cheese. In fact, unorthodox views are often best discovered from these unscheduled pit stops: such as an absorbing canvas of shimmering lakes covered in a flickering mist of brightly coloured dragon-flies and jumping fish. These whimsical scenes surely must have inspired Andersen's dreamlike fairy-tales. Certainly, Hans Christian's mother would despair at his love of dreaming up stories and idly recounting them to himself beneath the bough of a tree, rather than learning to read. He would imitate ballet dancers or acrobats while telling his tales, and memorise elaborate fantasies that he hoped would one day make it to a theatre or book. Driving the Garden Island route offers a compelling insight into Hans Christian's magical world: an idyllic country landscape scattered with enchanting stone castles where grand gated gardens remain steeped in the myth and legend of princes, princesses and elves.

From the unspoiled shores and dykes of Hasmark Strand, the trip to Odense Fjord is utterly beguiling. Drive first across an expanse of moorland vegetation, such as juniper, ling, heather and crow-berry. You'll see a narrow strip of pebble beach bordered by grass-fringed salt plains and reed swamps close to tumbledown cottages in vibrant Barbie-pink hues. Scour the scrubby terrain with care to seek out adders, grass snakes and sand lizards in an important resting place for Denmark's migratory bird species and a breeding ground for gulls, terns, herons and swans.

Funen's capital, Odense, offers more green space per head of population than any other city in the nation and boasts intimate shrub-fringed cobbled plazas and gardens filled with vibrant blooms. Park up (be selective where, to avoid a fine as hefty as a king's ransom) and enjoy a stroll along the winding Odense River, where shore-side jazz musicians serenade vessels that sail by. A dizzying array of cosy pavement cafes, bric-a-brac stalls and galleries offer the chance to pick up souvenirs and sustenance at the markets of Koncerthuset and Rosenbæk Gårdmarked. Odense's Hans Christian Andersen Museum celebrates the writer's entrancing tales, now translated into 150 languages around the world.

Drive on to share a glass of Denmark's tantalising bubbly, lovingly crafted by Sven Moesgaard and best enjoyed under one of Funen's oh-so-spectacular starry skies. Park up at majestic Egeskov Castle, and order a glass in the dimly lit bar that is so often filled with the symphonic thrills of Funen-born composer Carl Nielsen. The menu here is sumptuous and celebratory and a fitting reward for a sedate drive with minimal acceleration. Marvel as a zillion exploding fireworks dazzle Europe's most splendid 450-year-old moat castle amid a maze of towering hedges, herbaceous gardens, yew trees, grandiose fountains and fairy-shaped topiary – a tender setting.

Contacts:
Odense Tourist Bureau, Funen
www.visitodense.com

Visit Funen (Fyn)
www.visitfyn.com

THE AMALFI COAST, ITALY

With its pastel-hued villages terraced into steep hillsides, and precipitous corniche roads that curl around green-swathed mountains, the Amalfi Coast (Costiera Amalfitana) stretches high above turquoise waters and is Italy's most scenic shoreline stretch. Awarded a place on the UNESCO World Heritage list in 1997, this colourful coastal landscape is considered an outstanding example of a Mediterranean landscape with exceptional cultural and natural scenic values. Dramatic mountain cliffs rise up against sparkling seas on a mountainous terrain rich in sunlight as bright as the citrus fruits in the region's bountiful lemon groves. Narrow roads cling to the mountainside to keep pace with the winding curves of the shoreline. Drive this breathtaking road – by Alfa Romeo, Ferrari or Vespa – and you experience one of the most beautiful drives in the world.

Connecting Sorrento and Salerno, the Amalfi Coast spans a 60-kilometre (37-mile) coastal stretch just south of the Bay of Naples along the southern flanks of the jutting Sorrento Peninsula. It is a charismatic landscape, endowed with romantic views and timeless charm which deliver a sledgehammer to strike anyone arriving from Rome, or any other northern Italian city, on the Autostrada A1: the nation's bland spinal cord with its dark grey lanes. Amalfi, Positano and Ravello – historic heavyweights in literary, artistic and music terms – count among the most famous towns on Costiera Amalfitana (otherwise known as the SS163), with the most gasp-inducing drive arguably the 36-kilometre (22-mile) stretch between Positano's pebble-stone beaches and the ceramic-tiled buildings of Vietri sul Mare.

On a map, the town of Sorrento is revolver-shaped with the barrel and tip of the gun pointing inland away from the shore. When you drive through it, the impulse is to shoot straight down to the coast as the road is joyous, surrounded by hills, sun-bleached stone walls and fragrant citrus groves. It is an ambient town, full of quaint Italian pavement restaurants with their tables topped with bowls of olives, plump tomatoes, pasta dishes, bottles of buttery olive oil and tall carafes of wine. If you're lucky, you will find a parking spot outside the historic centre – otherwise head to the pricy main central car park, or take your chances on the outskirts of town. Grab a seat by the kerbside and order a platter of cold meats and smoked sausages to enjoy a typically long and leisurely lunch Italian-style – with a glass of limoncello, naturally.

Wedged into the side of the mountain, the colourful town of Positano is where Italy's jet-set gather. With its warm pastel tones and plethora of twinkling street lights, the town has a rich, warm glow in the last of the evening sun. It is home to some of the steepest staircases on Earth, which have been cut into the mountain; elderly locals nimbly ascend in a jiffy, but for tourists they're a lung-busting climb. Pretty backstreets

Photo: Miguel Hermoso Cuesta

are perfect for a shaded stroll or grab a zesty lemon gelato (ice cream) and head to one of the two little pebble beaches for views across the Li Galli archipelago, said to be where Ulysses was seduced by sirens.

Considered one of the most romantic and beautiful small towns in southern Italy, Ravello sits atop a steep, terraced slope. Wagner composed part of his opera *Parsifal* here in 1880 and this is also where author D.H. Lawrence wrote *Lady Chatterley's Lover.*

A wowzer stretch of corniche road passes by the Grotta dello Smeraldo not far from Praiano, a spectacular marine cave of luminous emerald waters that you can reach by boat, elevator or rock-cut steps. Praiano itself denotes an approximate half-way between Amalfi and Positano.

Though it is known more for its ships and maritime character, Amalfi is now a bustle of automobiles as one of the region's biggest shopping and tourist centres. Consequently it is synonymous with over-priced parking, whistle-tooting traffic officers and parking tickets. Once you have managed to park the car, be sure to stroll Amalfi and search out all the lovely alleyway shops and backstreet boutiques. Top buys are undoubtedly bottles of limoncello (the zingy lemon-infused liqueur) and delectable chocolate-dipped candied citrus peel – both specialities of the Amalfi Coast. Grab a coffee somewhere with a full sea view, *vista sul mare*, and let the deep-blue colour swallow you up as you fix your eyes on some unknown, distant point.

Famous as one of the main Allied beachheads during the 1943 invasion of Italy, Salerno is a village celebrated for its brightly painted ceramics. The road whisks you along some truly dramatic coastline, peppered with lookout points from which the utterly absorbing views can be imbibed.

Roads along the Amalfi Coast are famously winding

and narrow and can be tricky to navigate. Add to the mountainous slopes the drop-dead views and bravado of Italian drivers, night-time driving, in particular, can be a real challenge. If you can, do this drive in a small car; it'll take the curves better, stick to the narrow roads and be a heck of a lot easier to park. Scooters – the mode of transport of young Italians – buzz along the coast at speed; passing on the right, squeezing between your car and the mountains and scaring you half to death with random wobbles as they slow down. Avoid holding up traffic behind you – don't drive too fast, but don't drive too slow. Hug the walls and ease off the gas as you take a bend – there could be a larger vehicle or a tour bus the other side. Buses have the right of way, so let it get around first or slowly back up to allow it through. Watch out for fruit-sellers along the side of the road; they can sometimes reach out into the path of vehicles. If you can, avoid the crowds May to September – the Amalfi Coast is even more beautiful out of season when the roads are quiet.

BERLIN IN A PORSCHE 911

Famously modelled on the female form, the Porsche 911's seductive curves nip in at a waspish waist before round out to womanly contours. Synonymous with high-powered romance and glamour, to drive behind the wheel of a Porsche is to enter a dynamic world of power, prestige, playfulness and elegant poise. Porsche's manliness is embodied by a throaty engine rumble, while a slick, light-as-a-feather thrust evokes the aura of feminine grace. German-designed for pure driving enjoyment, a Porsche can be driven on every

type of road surface, rain or shine. No need to drive flat-out pedal to the metal; in order to experience its ultimate pleasures, simply touch, feel and absorb the unity of being wholly in-tune with the machine. Revved up by such stars as James Dean and Steve McQueen, Porsche's image is one of sensual glamour. Coax it into thrusting acceleration to pound the super-sleek German autobahns or idle along leafy country lanes to explore Berlin's romantic royal castles and storybook Gothic towers in style. According to Porsche purists, the more miles you cover in a 911, the deeper the affection grows – so settle back behind the steering wheel and let the love flow.

Unlike other high-performance sports cars, a Porsche is built to drive well under the mixed speed traffic conditions of a normal road, not just a speedway track. Germany's speedy superhighways allow plenty of opportunity to rip up the asphalt. However, a Porsche can potter around town and journey comfortably just as expertly as it can go from 0 to 60 in five-and-a-half seconds. Freezing sub-zero temperatures? No worries. A Porsche can also be left outside in the rain and snow overnight and will still purr like a cat in the morning.

Founded in the late 1940s by talented car designer Ferdinand Porsche, the basic marque has evolved through air-cooled 'flat six' engine 911 models to the latest water-cooled 996 (911) designs. Porsche remains a proud symbol of stylish German automotive ingenuity to be found in innumerable showrooms country-wide. Road-tripping weekenders keen to hit the freeway can also hire a Porsche 911 from a number of local car rental agencies, including Berlin's upscale division of Avis. Simply stump up around €200 a day and drive off the forecourt in the latest open-top model to journey to the city's little-known turrets, citadels, ruins, follies and palaces with the wind gently ruffling your hair.

Outer Berlin's landscape is straight from the Brothers Grimm: mysterious forests, medieval castles in the air and fabled rivers. Fairy-tale towers tell stories of ancient loves in enchanting, magical gardens dotted with sparkling lakes and spouting fountains. One of the most beautiful places in Berlin is Charlottenburg Palace. Originally named Lietzenburg, it had been commissioned by Sophie Charlotte, the wife of the Elector of Brandenburg, Friedrich III, but was renamed after her death. The original 17th-century Italian Baroque-style structure was expanded several times during the early 18th century to add an orangery and a new wing on the eastern side. Walks around the palace provide breathtaking views across the gardens to the mausoleum and the earlier tea house known as the Belvedere, which has some amazing collections of pottery and porcelain.

Other highlights that should form a part of any road-trip itinerary include Glienicke Palace, set amid an ensemble of parks, gardens and palaces created by the landscape architect Peter Joseph Lenné. Elements of Classical and Byzantine art and architecture are integrated into the palace and its gardens, underlining its Mediterranean character. Meander through spell-binding gardens to stunning riverside and lakeside walks to the Havel River. Gilt lions, modelled after the Villa Medici fountain in Rome, decorate a large fountain in front of the main façade, with the romantic leaf-shrouded *Klosterhof* (cloister yard) deserving of shared contemplation. It's the perfect place to unfurl a road-map and cogitate routes and ponder pit stops.

In the centre of Berlin, the 18th-century Prinzessin-nenpalais (the Palace of the Princesses, designed by Friedrich Wilhelm Dietrichs) has served as the residence for a number of different members of the Prussian ruling family. Almost destroyed during the Second World War, the palace has been restored to its former glory with a richly decorated interior and lavish opera hall. A short, enjoyable journey out to the Pankow district of the city allows an opportunity to witness one of Berlin's most marvellous examples of Baroque architecture, Schönhausen Palace, which is set in resplendent gardens near the Panke River. In 1740, Friedrich II gave this property to his wife, Elisabeth Christine, and much of the original furniture and decoration from this era remains. After the Second World War, the palace was used as the formal seat of the President of the GDR. Today, it is owned by the Prussian Palaces and Gardens Foundation Berlin-Brandenburg. Make your last port of call the sumptuously built Schlosshotel (Castle Hotel), a lavish former grand mansion and seat of the von Pannwitz family in 1914. Renowned throughout Germany for its extravagant banquets for 1,000 guests, waited on by 200 servants, today the Schlosshotel retains a rich, palatial charm evocative of bygone splendour. Karl Lagerfeld, the guru of haute couture, has placed his unmistakable signature on the stylish interior design. Thankfully the layout includes top-notch valet parking that ensures plenty of space in which to cosset a Porsche.

From central Berlin, a popular excursion with Porsche drivers is the 80-kilometre (50-mile) run out to Spreewald Forest on the city's south-eastern outer fringes. This UNESCO-designated biosphere reserve encompasses pine forest, alder trees, wetlands and sandy areas within its 648 square kilometres (250 square miles) and is flanked by nice, empty open roads.

Contacts:
Berlin Tourism
www.visitberlin.de

ITALY'S MILLE MIGLIA

Enzo Ferrari described the Mille Miglia as 'the world's greatest road race', and in the hearts and minds of Italian rally-car aficionados, he was spot on. Few events reflect the sheer passion of cars like that of the Mille Miglia – an ardour that remains even 80 years after its inception. Mix this gusto for fast engines with a zealous pursuit of adventure, excitement and discovery and the result is an open-road endurance race that epitomised the Gran Turismo buzz. On 26 March 1927, the first race started with around 75 starters – all Italian, and unlike modern-day rallying the slower cars set off first. In the early days of the race, most drivers set off before midnight and crossed the finishing line after dusk, if at all. The winner completed the course in 21 hours 5 minutes: a jaw-dropping time that sparked considerable awe.

Several specialised tour companies offer individually created itineraries to recapture the high-octane Mille Miglia thrill. From personally driving the latest model Ferrari and travelling for approximately 1,000 kilometres (620 miles) to accelerating through the steep, winding roads of Tuscany, packages are tailored to those who are keen to experience their own pedal-to-the-metal adrenaline rush. Most follow the figure-eight shaped course of roughly 1,500 kilometres (930 miles) of the legendary Mille Miglia rally to allow drivers to put their skills to the ultimate test. For example, a Ferrari event allows drivers to choose from a Ferrari 599 GTB Fiorano, Ferrari 430 Scuderia, Ferrari 430 Spider or a Ferrari 612 Scaglietti. Expert instructors then fully brief each driver on the peculiarities of each engine (eight-cylinder or twelve-cylinder) and give guidance on how to handle the

F1 paddle-gear shifting behind the steering wheel. Practice sessions prepare drivers for the power and might of their Ferrari before the route starts in earnest: a sensory at-the-wheel pleasure along an amazing succession of rolling hills and never-ending curves.

Of course, confident drivers with the right type of wheels could also enter the actual Mille Miglia itself – it's a relatively simple online application. It's not cheap (budget for around £6,500 to enter plus costs to get your car to Italy). You'll also need to allow for the cost of race prep, which may be considerable as the car will need to be in top order. The Mille Miglia doesn't provide mechanical support. This is a race and keeping the car running falls to you. Of course, as with any race of this pedigree, some cars are more eligible than others. With just 375 race slots available, these are always heavily over-subscribed. To avoid disappointment, increase your chances by entering a pre-war car (good), a relatively rare car (better) or a car that ran the Mille Miglia 'in period' (best). Of course, if you want a lock in an entry – and money is no object – you could always become a sponsor. Cars should be authentic (no replica cars permitted) and have a FIVA ID card. They also need to be inspected before the race – there are no exceptions. Applications should reach the Mille Miglia by mid-December so preparation for the event should begin at the end of the summer: you'll need top-notch photographs and the deadline is non-negotiable.

The Mille Miglia has signed directions in Italian only, so you'll need to brush up on the basics. Expect it to be chaos; it always is. It's 1,000 miles of chaos covering 40 towns in 48 hours – so if you can, appoint an Italian-speaking co-pilot to work a stopwatch, tell time, read a map and study the route. It also helps if they don't get car sick.

The route, from Brescia (Lombardi) to Rome (Lazio) via Firenze (Toscana), and back again, followed in the footsteps of races such as Targo Florio and the Carrera Panamericana to bring Alfa Romeo, Ferrari, Maserati and Porsche world-wide fame. Meaning 'thousand miles', the Mille Miglia took place 24 times from 1927 to 1957 and featured a host of big-name sport and touring cars. For the past 30 years or so, the event has been run as a retrospective event after the race was banned in 1957 after a fatal accident. From 1958 to 1961, the event resumed as a rallying-like round trip at legal speeds with a few special stages driven at full speed, but this was discontinued also. Today, a flashy showcase of flashy cars continues to draw millions of Italians out on to street corners, although the biggest cheers are reserved for the traditional pre-1957 models. This three-day show-stopping event is billed as the Mille Miglia Storica, a parade that includes a Mercedes-Benz 300 SLR from the 1950s and vintage Porsches dating back 40 years.

Although the starter's gun doesn't sound until early evening, it is fun to witness the 24-hour build-up first hand and wander among the other 374 of the world's most glamorous automobiles. En route to the race, stop at some of the highly prestigious car museums in Motor Valley, including those of Ferrari, Lamborghini, Maserati, Pannini and Ducati. Non-drivers can base themselves around one of the checkpoints on the route of the Mille Miglia for excellent race-day views – either south as it heads towards Rome or on the northbound sections. Hotel rooms in Lake Garda are booked solid around race time because it is a great place to watch the Mille Miglia's final stages. Or try Brescia, where the finishing line is located, the ultimate post-race party venue with an incredible atmosphere welcoming drivers safely home.

Contacts:
Mille Miglia
www.1000miglia.eu

Italian Tourist Board
www.italiantouristboard.co.uk

AFRICA

THE DRAA VALLEY, MOROCCO

For centuries, the Draa Valley has been a byword for bountiful, plentiful crops because it is here that the fertile waters from the Dadès River and Imini River meet and irrigate the rich, surrounding soil. Fresh from the High Atlas mountains, the waters flow south-east to Tagounite before meandering slowly westward towards the Atlantic Ocean, leaving well-nourished fields of plump fruit, vegetables and flowers in their wake. The Drawi people have long revered the river waters that bring such riches to their land: a picturesque valley of rugged volcanic rock that was once one of the old caravan routes that brought treasures to the sultans.

Driving in Morocco means braving the heat and swirling dust that are omnipresent around every tiny town and village. Parched settlements blasted with scorching winds are scattered with grit-resistant camels. The desert sands are just part of this achingly beautiful region that incorporates dramatic rocky gorges, lush green oases and wildly colourful small towns. Until the early 20th century, the Draa Valley was criss-crossed by caravan trails that ferried vast riches to Morocco's spoiled sultans. Today, some of these routes can still be traced in countryside dotted with donkeys and goats. Children run across fields to play among mud-brick ruins and sacks laid with drying dates. Domed mosques peek out from hilltop villages, above winding rivers that were once infested by thousands of crocodiles, and where chickens peck at dried-out corn on dusty scrub.

Every sound the car makes echoes throughout the hills, mountains and meadows of the Draa Valley, despite the constant movement of livestock and children. In bygone times, this region was alive with merchants and traders carrying cloth, spices, weapons and other riches. Many of the caravans made their way to the great slave markets at Fez or Marrakesh, others sold to rural land owners who would put their slaves to work in the fields. Today, in the Draa Valley, many people you meet on your journey proudly claim to be the descendants of slaves, especially in the areas around the market town of Agdz, referred to as the Door to the Draa Valley. Stallholders here are Haritine people, selling dates and palm baskets from rickety wooden tables. Their forefathers were black descendants from the West African region of Mali: according to legend, when the 19th-century caravans passed through, date palms sprung up among henna fields, water wells and lush gardens along the trails they travelled.

In Tansikht there are plenty of local Berber families happy to serve travellers a traditional meal, often as part of cooking lessons. I had been in town less than ten minutes when Omar made my acquaintance. My stomach rumbled impatiently as he described the traditional bread and a tajine that his mother had planned for lunch that day. Omar asked his mother to set

Photo: Richard Allaway

another place at the table and took me for a stroll around the village to meet his coffee-shop kin. We bought fresh produce at the market. 'Everything has been picked this morning', he explained with pride. 'Our green fields are full of herbs and vegetables.' The approach to his mother's house took us through a traditional Berber neighbourhood – complete with the earthy smell and noise of livestock mingled with the musk and amber of home-grown spices. Swirls of smoke from a griddle pan filled the small strip of kitchen in Omar's home. It was as hot as Hades and the air was thick with *ras el hanout* (a fragrant mix of up to 100 spices), sweet citrus and apricots. While we waited for a pan of couscous to simmer and a giant flat-bread to bubble and puff, we shared a bowl of ink-black salty olives. Clattering pots and pans rang like bells as Omar started to pass plates around. The floor was set with oversized cushions. Hungrily, we scooped up a delicious lunch using strips of bread and our hands. There were at least half-a-dozen platters of spice-rich tajine of lamb, tomatoes and pulses – a feast of orange, red and yellow.

The road snakes through the Draa Valley, linking Agdz and M'Hamid and passing through Zagora. Progress is modest in the Draa as the road slowly skirts the fertile band in the middle of an immense desert limestone plateau. But time seems meaningless in a land of flowering oases, orchards and rustling palm groves. For spectacular sweeping views across a broad panorama of the Draa Valley, take the Tinififft mountain pass from Ouarzazate, then the P31 road towards Zagora. After 60 kilometres (37 miles) it climbs up the flanks of the Jebel Tifernine to the pass at more than 1,600 metres (5,249 feet) – so get ready to point your camera over the peaks of the Sahro for a world-beating snap. Another loop that bamboozles the eyes with colour is the road that leads through the Draa from a point just after the

Tansikht Bridge. It snakes its way through the flower-filled meadows of the valley past adobe villages to Zagora (taking around three or four hours). Further on from Tansikht, there's an alternative route for intrepid types with a sturdy 4×4. The roughshod trail on the right quickly transports you to a lunar landscape that stretches from the Jebel Rhart to Zaouia Tafechna. When the road forks into two, take the left for Tazzarine and go straight to reach Zagora (again, a three-or-four-hour trip).

Contacts:
Morocco Tourist Board
www.visitmorocco.com

SKELETON COAST ROUTE, NAMIBIA

Though the name alone can send shivers down the spines of those unacquainted with its history, the Skeleton Coast along the stark shoreline of Namibia isn't as ghoulish as it may sound. In years gone by, an abundance of giant whale carcasses would wash up along the shore here, their bones picked clean by scavenging wildlife. To passing mariners it was an eerie sight and the coast's alabaster skeletons were enough to cause panic throughout the crew. Numerous ships came to grief here, due to the strong currents and swirling fogs of this Atlantic coastline. This added human skeletons to the toll of bones, further fuelling the dark superstitions of this unusual coastal wilderness. In 1933 news journalist Sam Davis dubbed the region 'the Skeleton Coast' to add theatre and the name stuck. Davis had been reporting on the search for a Swiss airman, Carl Nauer, whose plane had disappeared while trying to break the Cape Town to London solo air record. No trace of him or the plane was ever found. Today the name seems apt, as it has a high death tally – a harsh desert, wide-open space, isolation and challenging conditions have seen to that. Because of the low traffic volumes, roads are not tarred here, hence the series of hellishly bumpy, partially made roads – the C34, the D2302 and the D39 – that run for around 500 kilometres (311 miles) along the Skeleton Coast from south of the Orange River to the border with Angola. Encompassing the whole Namibian coastline, the Skeleton Coast Park is sparsely populated with considerable landscape, animal and plant diversity.

Now more about the partially made roads.

Almost all of the first 200 kilometres (124 miles) of road – to the Ugab Gate, the entry point for the southern section of the Skeleton Coast Park – is laid with a sand-and-salt mix. Vegetation has been scythed away, bladed to earth level, then compacted over time by traffic. These ungraded tracks are laid where a daily use of less than five vehicles is expected. The earth is layered with a concentrated salt-water and gypsum-rich material that is dangerously slippery in almost all weathers but is particularly perilous following a heavy coastal mist. In the rare event that it rains, all journeys are off. Even in daylight, drivers are asked to keep their headlights on to ensure other vehicles know they are there, especially oncoming cars. Zero traction on the road surface makes this route almost impossible for anything other than a 4×4.

Namibia has a relatively high prevalence of road accidents relative to its sparse population – most are caused by roaming wild animals, the driver's loss of concentration or falling asleep at the wheel. Maintaining the road to keep it in a serviceable condition costs the Road Authority a fortune. Drivers also face a hefty bill when it comes to cleaning accumulated salt and mud from their cars – it coats the paintwork like thick, dirty glue and clogs up every filter and cog. On the hottest days, a heavy hazy heat hangs in the air like damp washing along the Skeleton Coast. Humidity can soar suddenly when the wind (Oosweer) blows from the inland plains. Sandstorms erupt and the effect is suffocating, as what is left of the air is filled with a zillion particles of grit, dust and sand. Heat-induced hallucinations (mirage effect) and fatal dehydration are both common when sky, sea and horizon blur into one shimmering visual chaos. When a thick blanket of fog sits on the coast, stretching as far as 16 kilometres (10 miles) inland, navigation is impossible. Even with a compass, you'll get hopelessly lost.

Fuel stops are infrequent, so be sure to fill up before departure – not just your tank but jerrycans too. The locals use all readily available receptacles: coke bottles, buckets, the lot. For several kilometres, driving behind a clapped-out beat-up old banger with a roof patched up with packing tape and string, I'd never been more terrified, having spotted the men sitting in the back smoking surrounded by around 50 gallons of fuel. With ash-heavy glowing cigarettes clamped between their lips, the men chatted over open vessels of petrol. The whole vehicle – if not an entire square mile – was an incendiary tinderbox, moments away from fireballing. I was mightily relieved when the truck pulled over for a break, just as one of the men struck a match again.

Though it is easy to romanticise the drive along this lonely terrain, covered in an ever-shifting swirling carpet of sand, it can be hostile and bleak. Signposts are sporadic on the Skeleton Coast Road and can be a source of confusion: while Namibia has used the metric system for almost half a century, distances along the Skeleton Coast are signed in miles. Road

Photo: Laika ac

conditions aren't signed – so sinkholes, deep ruts and the sharp rock splinters of the gravel sections can often cause real damage. Two spare wheels are recommended – if you can carry more, do.

Eco-signs on the C34 will warn you to stay on the road – and the Road Authority enforces this rule. Due to the vulnerable and highly fragile ecosystem here, east of Swakopmund on the gravel plains, off-roading is strictly prohibited. Vehicles cause untold damage to rare lichen, endangered plants and desert fauna and a single vehicle track is likely to remain visible for hundreds of years. As one of the first plant forms that evolved from the ancient oceans of the Ordovician period, lichens are an extremely hardy plant that grow in the world's rocky arid surfaces, from the Polar Regions to the tropics. They provide protection for the ground surface from water and wind erosion and are a critical part of the evolutionary process. There is very little evidence of the oil and diamond extraction that has taken place here. Mining projects have been scrapped almost as soon as they've started: wells are dry and gems are few and far between. I spotted an old dumper truck part-buried in the sand, but the other relics are further up the coast.

The Skeleton Coast National Park is set into two distinctly separate 8,000-hectare (19,768-acre) zones: the southern zone is a 210-kilometre (130-mile)-long coastal strip between the Ugab River in the south and the Hoanib River in the north. The northern section of the park extends 290 kilometres (180 miles) from the Hoanib River to the Kunene River on the Angolan border. At about 187 kilometres (116 miles) you will arrive at Ugab Gate, the southern entry point. North of the Ugab Gate the C34 becomes a gravel stretch. Sand dunes of different colours flank the roadside, from pale ivory and yellow gold to sooty black. It's hard to imagine that these are what the colonial-era Portuguese once called the 'Sands of Hell' as they look simply magical – especially against the grey rocks clung with bright orange lichen. Windswept stubby plants, stunted and thickened, can survive here for long periods without moisture. When it does rain, birders flock to the shore to watch birds feeding among the coastal delta – a place that was once desolate and barren is no longer devoid of life. Deep within the park environments is the only overnight stop, a simple state-run lodge camp, Terrace Bay. About six hours' drive north of Swakopmund, the camp was once part of a mining operation that went bankrupt. Outside of the park, on a 3,000-square-kilometre (1,158-square-mile) private reserve by the dry Khumib River is the Skeleton Coast Camp – a deluxe alternative. Stay in upscale tents and enjoy exploring the area with an expert guide who'll introduce you to desert-adapted elephants, a colony of 250,000 cape fur seals and ancient stone circles. To see the Skeleton Coast through his eyes was, for me, an utterly compelling reason to take a day's rest from the driver's seat – his enthusiasm was infectious.

Contacts:
Namibia Tourist Board
www.namibiatourism.com.na

LIMPOPO RIVER ROUTE, SOUTH AFRICA

Zigzagging in an enormous arc, the Limpopo is a typically sluggish heavily silted African river famous for its aggressive hippopotamus population. Rudyard Kipling immortalised the Limpopo in his *Just So* stories, describing it as 'the great grey-green, greasy Limpopo River, all set about with fever trees'. It forms a border for about 640 kilometres (398 miles) with a trio of nations: South Africa to the south-east, Botswana to the north-west and Zimbabwe to the north. For this reason, many road-trippers aspire to journey the Limpopo Route as, like most border regions, it represents an exciting fusion of cultures. Seven of South Africa's eleven official languages are spoken here – and that's not counting all the variances and dialects. Travel through Limpopo and you'll also meet people from the majority of South Africa's ethnic groups, from Zulu and Xhosa to the Shangana or Tsonga, the Ndebele, the Venda and the Northern Sotho. Different faces, distinctive physical characteristics and a medley of unique foods, traditions, beliefs, music, dance, celebrations and superstitions wait to be discovered – all in one invigorating road-trip.

Running from South Africa's tip, Limpopo Province honours the country's second-biggest river (total length 1,600 kilometres/994 miles). Once it has flowed slowly through South Africa, Botswana, Mozambique and Zimbabwe, it spills into the warm waters of the Indian Ocean. In the South African portion alone, more than 5 million people live close to the Limpopo River in a landscape of mixed savannah grasslands and trees. With over 50 provincial reserves and several luxury game reserves, including the famous Limpopo National Park, Limpopo Province is also home to Mapungubwe Cultural Landscape, one of South Africa's eight UNESCO World Heritage sites. As South Africa's first kingdom, Mapungubwe was a pre-colonial state (1075–1220) located at the confluence of the Shashe and Limpopo Rivers. It prospered into the subcontinent's largest realm, before it was abandoned in the 14th century. During this period, gold and ivory were traded with China, India and Egypt and the population of Mapungubwe swelled to more than 5,000 people. Parts of the province remain unchanged by time, remaining inhospitably hot and covered in tangled thornbush. Others have been brutally modernised in the name of progress: traffic roars up and down the busy N1 highway that splits the province in two. Yet venture into the wilderness areas with their mountainous landscapes and vast open spaces and you'll see wildlife galore. For here is where the country's highest population of rhinos is found, as well several species of antelope. And as the home of the world-famous Kruger National Park, there is first-class game-viewing to be had.

Limpopo is a more authentic, less sanitised version of Southern Africa. In among the incredible flora and fauna – much of it used in medicinal cures and aromatic therapies – you'll find rustic village settlements set around livestock pens and sun-parched scrub. Children play games in the dusty ground surrounded by scrawny chickens and women stir bubbling brew-pots filled with slow-cooked goat. The scene forms a sharp contrast to the city of Johannesburg: the start of most road-trips into Limpopo. After just over three hours on the N1 freeway, I arrived at the malaria-free Welgevonden Game Reserve for a three-night African safari experience among giraffe, kudu, zebra, eland and impala. Welgevonden means 'well found' in Dutch and I'm rather pleased that I did, deep in the Waterberg plateau, just north of Johannesburg's urban sprawl. On the N1 it was an easy drive to the R33 off-ramp. Once I'd navigated the toll, I joined the weaving grasslands on the R510 to Welgevonden, where it's a Big Five hangout. Elephants, rhinos, lions, leopards and buffalo thrive, along with an abundance of bird life. In fact, in total there are 50 different mammals – including rare and

Photo: Hansueli Krapf

unusual species, such as brown hyena, pangolin, aardwolf and aardvark – that are all best seen at night.

I grabbed a beer, cracked it open by the tented camp and supped it from a lookout deck while I studied the resplendent knotted bushveld in front of me for signs of its prolific bird life. Rolling wooded mountains cut by deep rocky ravines and majestic gorges make this a highly evocative piece of Africa – a place of rare and rugged beauty. Over the next few days, out on the grassy plains, I was privileged to get up close to an eland and a pride of lions. In the dry, long grass we found evidence of leopards and caught sight of well over two dozen of the 300 bird species found in Welgevonden, including rare blue cranes. At 34,850 hectares (86,116 acres) in size, you could easily spend a week or more exploring this magnificent reserve – there's so much to see and do in this unique wilderness, which only allows a limited number of guests at any one time. No private vehicles are permitted to ensure minimal human impact on the landscape and its wildlife. Historically, wildlife on the reserve has never been hunted, so game-viewing is always up close, intimate and exclusive.

From here, my car takes me along a striking stretch of the N1 where I'm blessed with views of indigenous tree species. There are lots of inviting walking trails, where it's possible to stroll among incredible African wildlife including giraffe, zebra, wildebeest, porcupines and pangolins. I'm heading to the Mapungubwe National Park to learn more about Africa's earliest kingdom. The first black Africans arrived in South Africa across the Limpopo River some time before AD 300 and established themselves in a settlement here. With such strong historical and cultural ties, Mapungubwe is a hotbed of traditional arts and crafts such as pottery and woodcarving. Ancient customs are still an important part of life. Witchcraft and age-old medicine are still commonly practised. I'm now about 530 kilometres (329 miles) north of my start point in Johannesburg, near the Botswana border. I'm in a 4×4, so can drive the whole 135 kilometres (84 miles) through the park – only 35 kilometres (22 miles) are accessible to normal 2WD vehicles. Mapungubwe is not a safari destination primarily, but a cultural and historical site – though as I enjoy a fascinating walk through South African history it is impossible not to be bowled over by the park's real wilderness appeal. I see elephant, blue wildebeest, Burchell's zebra and warthog from various viewing points on boulders and rocky outcrops as the wildlife ventures to drink from pools and rivers that haven't disappeared in the heat. The Heritage Walk is utterly absorbing and offers real historical insight into this great ancient kingdom and the gold rhino found here. If you've not seen a giant Baobab tree before, this is also a great place to spot the distinctive swollen trunk. Storing massive amounts of water in their stems to cope with seasonal droughts, the Baobab's fruits are large pods rich in vitamin C known as 'monkey bread' or 'cream of tartar fruit'. Renowned for their massive circumference, this mammoth tree species can achieve a girth of over 45 metres (148 feet) – roughly the equivalent of 25 people standing with hands linked. You can visit the biggest ever 'Big Baobab' in the Limpopo Province, a tree that has been carbon dated as well over 1,700 years old and that has even made the front page of the *Wall Street Journal*! When Baobabs age, they begin to hollow inside. The Limpopo Big Baobab is on the Sunland mango farm, set among beautiful waterfalls and biking trails, and is a very special tree house. Not only does it provide shelter and food for numerous birds and animals but it also doubles as a saloon bar (with enough room for 60 guests) and is nourished by the mighty Limpopo River.

Contacts:
South African Tourist Board
www.southafrica.net

THE GARDEN ROUTE, SOUTH AFRICA

Spanning one of the most beautiful stretches of coastline, the Garden Route runs alongside the Outeniqua Choo-Tjoe Garden Railway following the route around Africa's southernmost tip. Though the Garden Route tag is a bit of a misnomer (this isn't a gardener's dream vacation strewn with horticultural thrills), this densely vegetated region of South Africa is rich in diverse natural beauty. Comprising 200 kilometres (124 miles) of indigenous temperate forest beneath the ragged peaks of the Tsitsikamma and Outeniqua mountains, it runs alongside rocky coves and glorious sandy beaches and is dotted with gorges, lakes and lagoons. The Garden Route, in many ways, has little of the wilder feel of the 'real' Africa about it, yet with excellent tourist infrastructure, arts and crafts galleries and good restaurants it is a pleasure to drive. Choose scenic 'Route 62' or the more functional N2, depending on how much time you have to meander.

The most obvious gateway to the Garden Route is Cape Town, about four hours' drive away. Running all the way to a bungee-jump bridge in Storms River, the route spans a host of scenic destinations such as Wilderness National Park and Plettenberg Bay wedged between the Indian Ocean and three mountain ranges. Offering the mighty majesty of elephants on land and whales close to the shore, the Garden Route is blessed with a near-perfect climate with cool, wet winters and temperate summers, ensuring the fertile soils of the region produce some of South Africa's most fantastic wines. Swirling a luscious plum-coloured full-bodied Pinotage around a glass to breathe in the deep aromas of raspberries and black cherries is heavenly under South African sunshine. The sound of melodic birdsong echoes around a corridor of leafy vines. Hundreds of winegrowers include well-known names such as Jakkalsvlei Vineyards in the Langeberg Mountains, Bramon Wine Estate in The Crags and Herold Wine in George – all of which welcome visitors keen to taste and buy.

Road-trippers are spoilt for choice when it comes to choosing a hire car to drive from Cape Town, so if you fancy motoring down the N2 in an open-topped MGB roadster or astride a Harley Davidson, this route is for you. Self-drive car rental is cheap and the roads are top-notch. However, as I'm planning to drop into several wineries – and I know that South African wine glasses are generous (and refills numerous) – I'm road-tripping the Garden Route in the passenger seat. We have a spontaneous itinerary on the dashboard but plan to keep it flexible, loose and unmapped.

Pass dinky little beach towns and seaside parlours by the shore, pretty little bays with glassy waters and gentle surf home to astounding numbers of sharks. We stopped off for fresh juices and home-ground coffee at Hermanus, a lovely little town that claims it is the easiest place in the world to spot whales from land between July to January each year. Dark-green hills with velvety folds and shaggy meadows and lollypop trees flanked the road on one side with fall-away slopes down to the sea on the other. After sipping delicious wines and eating springbok pies under a stove-hot gold-and-blue sky, we gently motored inland to the sleepy town of Swellendam. Nestled at the base of the mountains,

Photo: Rian Wall

with horseback riding trails and waterfall cascades, this backroad settlement is a stop-over for anyone keen to explore some of South Africa's most beautiful countryside. Before a supper of man-size slabs of beef cooked over a BBQ (*brai*), we were invited to taste four superb wines in the cellars of a small, independent local producer for a shoestring price. On the way back to our B&B lodge, we skipped over spring grass, jumped across streams and marvelled at how joyous Chardonnay in glasses the size of bath tubs can make you feel.

After gunning down the mountains at a fair old lick, we arrived in Sedgefield just in the nick of time to catch the pink-and-amber-glow of a gorgeous sunset in Plettenberg Bay (known as 'Plett' by the locals). We dined like kings on barbecued sausages (*boerewors roosterkoek*) on the sands while marvelling at the clarity of the night sky. As a port of call, Plettenberg Bay takes some beating – I honestly could have stayed here among its hammock strung trees and powdery sands forever. Despite the flashy hotels of this seaside resort, including The Lodge with its upscale Phillippe Starck bathrooms, there's also plenty of good-value family accommodation – lots with idyllic sea views. There are some excellent dive schools here, so if you've time book an underwater trip to see soft corals, sharks, parrotfish and the indigenous Knysna seahorse.

For a wilder, woollier adventure, take the N2 to journey east of Plett along a steep descent through old-growth forest on a twisting road to Nature's Valley, where you'll find an empty rustic beach and unspoilt lagoon. Beyond Nature's Valley lies a fine stretch of unruly coastline, in beautiful Tsitsikamma National Park. Numerous adventure sports, crazy-paced hiking and other adrenaline-pumping pursuits are found here, together with empty beaches, relaxing sunrises, incredible sunsets and fine wines and food. Follow countless trekking, biking and riding trails as well as one of South Africa's best long-distance hikes, the 42-kilometre Otter Trail, offering five days of superb coastal walking with rivers to ford and plenty of time to swim, snorkel or just relax in one of the simple, wooden overnight huts. Though the Garden Route is not prime safari territory, there are some opportunities to visit classic African game lodges from here. It's not much of a detour to also make a trip out to the elephants at Greater Addo National Park. You can also push inland from Plett, crossing the Outeniqua Mountains via the dramatic unpaved Prince Alfred's Pass, or take the asphalted stretch from George up to Oudtshoorn. Either will bring you to the dusty, sun-baked landscape of the Little Karoo with its bygone charm. From here it is easy to reach the celebrated wine-growers in the Breede River Valley and Cape Winelands.

From Swellendam to Sedgefield, the journey transports you across the ridge roads of the mountains into dusty desert – a trip that takes you deep into the heart of the Karoo on famous Route 62.

At Oudtshoorn the madcap antics of a population of ostriches baffled us, pecking furiously at anything in their way and sprinting round in crazy circles. A sign proclaiming Oudtshoorn as the 'ostrich capital of the world' helps make sense of it all. These bizarre, aggressive feathered beasts are nothing compared with our next activity – cage diving with enormous crocodiles. I'm not sure any other country in the world offers the opportunity to enjoy an eyeball-to-eyeball encounter with a 12-foot gap-toothed crocodile in this way. If it does, I'm not convinced I'd try it again. From within a submerged rustic cage the size of a public phone kiosk, the prospect of a death-plunge with a prehistoric species was both thrilling and terrifying. However, the excitement of it all soon dissipated when the terror took hold. And fifteen minutes in the enclosure with a massive reptile with hundreds of razor sharp teeth and a killer mentality was quite long enough – even though the guys that ran the joint assured me the croc was very well-fed. Controlled by an overhead monorail the feeling of dangling, suspended above the crocs, caused my legs to turn to jelly. Never had a glass of wine that evening been more deserved! There's more terror to be had in the coal-black Cango Caves, near Oudtshoorn – best avoided by anyone scared of the dark. Strike deep into hot, airless, inner recesses, along skinny claustrophobic craggy passages, eventually pulling yourself up the other side to breathe fresh air under the Garden Route's blue skies dotted with cotton-wool clouds.

Contacts:
South African Tourist Board
www.southafrica.net

AUSTRALASIA

GREAT OCEAN ROAD, AUSTRALIA

When I first drove this road, I knew nothing of its history. So I toured it with the wind in my hair, feeling giddy on the freedom that epic Australian road-trips bring. It felt so liberating to have the pedal to the metal on such a glorious, expansive stretch of coastline. Just me, a station wagon and 243 kilometres (151 miles) of open road.

By the time I drove it again, the trip had greater poignancy as I'd learned the historic significance of this stunning ocean route. Built by returned soldiers of the First World War, the Great Ocean Road was hacked out of rugged rocks as a permanent memorial to their colleagues who'd died while fighting. Skirting the once isolated southern coast, this extraordinary engineering feat revolutionised travel between Lorne and Geelong, once an extremely long and arduous rough coach track ride. Boats had previously been the primary link to the outside world for places like Lorne and Geelong.

Though plans for an ocean road were proposed as early as 1880, they only gained real impetus towards the end of the First World War. As part of a programme of repatriation and re-employment of returned soldiers, the idea of road creation in sparsely populated areas took hold. Originally called the 'South Coast Road', the route had changed its name to the Great Ocean Road Trust before it came to fruition. As a lasting monument to those who had died in the war, the Government at the time had a powerful view of its worth as a tourist attraction, proclaiming it better for its ocean, mountain, river and fern gully scenery than the Riviera in France, the San Francisco Road and Bulli Pass in New South Wales.

After the horrors of the First World War, thousands of returned soldiers descended on the southern coast to take on back-breaking work. Using horse-pulled carts – for there was no heavy machinery – 3,000 men hacked at the rock with picks, shovels and axes. It took almost fourteen years to complete. Construction began in September 1919 and by then the route had altered to cut through the bush and

Photo: Camille Gerstenhaber

rock from Lorne to Warrnambool. On 26 November 1932 the route was officially opened by a procession of 40 cars. Flag-waving schoolchildren lined sections of the road and a special ceremony took place at the memorial arch. By the time it opened, the route formerly known as the B100 had cost £81,000. Funded by private contributions and borrowing, the construction costs were repaid from toll collection in Great Ocean Road's earliest years. The road was gifted to the state in 1936.

Today, the Great Ocean Road is not just simply a beautiful road-trip that makes your heart sing. It is also the largest First World War memorial in the world. In 2011, the road was added to the Australian National Heritage List and its place in history is now officially assured. Every year the Great Ocean Road Marathon, a world-renowned Festival of Running, is staged on the 44-kilometre (27-mile) section of the road, from Lorne to Apollo Bay.

A popular extended 'tour route' is touted to visiting road-trippers like me – and it's a joy. It takes in the Great Ocean Road's many side roads and excursions, acknowledging that it is a gateway to other regional attractions, such as Geelong and the Bellarine Peninsula, the Great Otway National Park and the Shipwreck Coast. This longer version totals 665 kilometres (413 miles), starting in Australia's second city Melbourne and ending in the fishing village of Port Fairy. On this route, sightseers at the wheel will pass rainforests, vineyards, world-class surfing breaks, seaside towns and eucalyptus trees, bird-topped limestone cliffs, heathlands, pocket-sized beaches and cattle ranches.

From downtown Melbourne, the start of the Great Ocean Road is a scenic hour's drive to the seaside town of Torquay. Here you'll find a sign denoting the route's official beginning, together with Australia's top surf hangouts, including oh-so-cool Bell's Beach, host of the annual Rip Curl Pro. On a route as mellow and meandering at the Great Ocean Road stretch, there is plenty of opportunity to taste farm-fresh produce, seafood and cool-climate wines. Tour operators all along the Great Ocean Road offer a range of exciting excursions, including scuba diving on wrecks and reefs, sea-kayaking and hiking, guided wildlife walks to spot kangaroos and forest birds, and fishing in rivers and lakes. Specialist operators also offer full-on three- or four-day hiking expeditions such as the magnificent 104-kilometre (65-mile) Great Ocean Walk. Numerous points en route offer a wide variety of overnight accommodation from dirt cheap campsites and budget motels to self-catering apartments, high-end hotels and spa resorts.

A whole gamut of activity choices and sightseeing options makes this a great route for an independent traveller. Whatever vehicle you have – jeep, motorhome, motorbike or bicycle – you'll find this road-trip a breeze. Family groups are sure to love the safe roads, the food joints and the whale-, dolphin- and platypus-spotting trips; teens the cool surf bars, the beach scene and the adventure sports; honeymooners the empty sands, the luxury boutique B&Bs and top-notch gastronomy. This really is the road-trip for everyone. Even pets.

The biggest risk on this trip? It's rushing the experience: an all-too-common mistake. Oh, and if you're keen to avoid the crowds and feel the space of a coastal road don't visit during school holidays, especially the long summer break (December to January).

Contacts:
Australian Tourist Board
www.visitaustralia.com

TASMANIA, AUSTRALIA

Motoring around Tasmania is a seductive proposition – a chance to explore the unworldly terrain of a wave-carved island blessed with old-growth eucalyptus and golden button-grass moorlands. Drive here, and you're traversing a land packed with hundreds of miles of dolerite cliffs, root-riddled emerald forests and glacial valleys virtually untroubled since the last Ice Age. The fact that it can claim to be the Southern Hemisphere's last terrestrial expanse adds further intrigue. As an island off the shore of a continent, Tasmania has the feel of raw isolation – even though the split from mainland Australia was around 12,000 years ago. Part of this is a conscious eco-struggle to retain some of the last feral wildernesses on Earth. Mystical geological attributes, untamed moss-clad woodlands, soaring ferns and an oddball assortment of bizarre creatures are an intrinsic part of Tasmania. Much of the island has been protected by the statutes of UNESCO since 1982. So to travel Tasmania is to journey through a triumph of Mother Nature and her jewel-box of natural treasures.

At roughly the same size as Switzerland, Tasmania offers road-trippers some easy wins. The western coast is spectacular. Tasmania is also remarkably crowd-free. Roads appear almost empty. No roar of traffic. No speeding cars forcing me into the gutter. No spewing diesel fumes. Hobart is the island's capital, yet it has a small-town feel. Though it boasts the distinction of being Australia's most rain-drenched state, the sun shines brightly. It felt good to climb into the open-topped ute and pull on to the open road. Hobart's clapboard houses and Georgian sandstone buildings were behind me now. An unfurled map stretched across the passenger seat – next stop Launceston!

A crash of gears pushed us along the 80-kilometre (50-mile) route north-west from Hobart to the sleepy town of Hamilton. Everywhere was awash with vibrant colour and the relentless visual stimulation was bamboozling. From what I could gather, I was rattling alongside a disused railway line: a route that switched without warning from sleek asphalt to an unpaved stretch. After a succession of bumps, the countryside served as a distraction: the yellow-green pasture looked like plush velour embroidered with silken wildflowers. Squiggly S-shaped creeks and lush valleys characterised the undulating stretch to New Norfolk, before Bushy Park's handsome oast houses and hop fields, reminiscent of Kent in southern England. By the time I reached Hamilton, a charming limestone settlement blessed with 1830s faded good looks, my legs demanded a stretch. The town, built almost entirely by convict labour, makes an excellent base from which to trek the leafy trails of Mount Field National Park.

It felt good to hurtle along a route free of congestion. I even enjoyed the smallest country backroads with their potholes, lumps and bumps. My map rustled to a comforting pulsing rhythm as I bounced up and down in my seat. Not even the syncopated clanging of some minor mechanical mishap under the bonnet could spoil the mood. One beautiful village led to another in a heady scenic blur. Wrenching the wheel on a tight switchback, I noticed the miles were passing effortlessly. North from Hamilton, I set my sights on Tarraleah and earmarked Ouse in the Central Highlands of Tasmania for a pit-stop. Here a strong Scots heritage prevails. There is a *Brigadoon*-style feel to mist-shrouded Ouse, set among windswept bristly trees. Just a few hardy souls live in the slatted wooden homes, working the blood-red soil of the land. With a whine of protestation,

Photo: Plug

the ute slow-burnt up a steep incline and did the automotive version of an exhausted pant on reaching the top. I peered down at an inky-green river rich in trout, allowing a few minutes engine recovery time. Then the ute and I enjoyed a jalopy-style descent, crashing through shallow streams as if tipsy on peace and quiet. At times, the only audible sound, other than the engine, was my own breath. Being so silent is a strangely spiritual experience. It felt disrespectful to switch the radio on, so I didn't.

A picnic area in Tarraleah provided a good opportunity to eat and stroll. Using a tree stump as a makeshift table, I snacked on thick slices of bread and leatherwood honey before exploring a short woodland trail and discovering magnificent birds of prey. Back in the ute, I took a wrong turn but enjoyed a tarmac mystery tour in which I survived a series of gruelling hills and a rapid descent from Mount Arrowsmith. Another roller-coaster road deposited me at an old mining district on the slopes of Mount Owen, where a white-knuckle 6-kilometre (4-mile) downhill stretch contains 99 terrifying bends. It is impossible not to whoop with joy at the monster-sized ferns in a zillion hues of green at the bottom.

Pottering around Strahan's pretty harbour brings a chance to snap up some oyster-shell knick-knacks as souvenirs. Then it's a downhill chase from Mount Murchison before following Cradle Mountain's jagged contours from the northern end of a spectacular national park, Lake St Clair. Famous for its fearsome dolerite peaks, dense rainforest and varicoloured beech trees riddled by icy streams, this extraordinary expanse boasts a wildlife-rich cool temperate rainforest set against steep mountain slopes. The famous Overland Track begins from here: a demanding feat of physical endurance and one of Australia's premier wilderness walks. Jeeps ferry hikers back and forth along this ice-age swathe, dotted with caves, quarries, basalt plains and Pleistocene archaeological sites. Some of the world's largest carnivorous marsupials inhabit these regions, including the spotted-tailed quoll and the eastern quoll – two of the world's only three surviving monotremes. I, however, have my eyes peeled for an elusive Tasmanian devil, a creature rarely seen by humans in the wild. Since a rare cancer decimated numbers, this unique beast has almost disappeared. It remains unclear whether the Tasmanian devil will survive the epidemic or, like the Tasmanian tiger, will disappear into the world of legend and myth. I scoured the forest for a stocky, black-and-white-flecked dog-like creature with a large boxy head – and kept my fingers crossed.

Leaving the banks of the Meander River behind, the ute and I rumbled through level plains of crimson poppy fields. Next on the map were the pinprick towns of Exton, Hagley, Carrick and Hadspen, though I'd earmarked Westbury in which to take a break. According to the travel guide, this elegant English-style town boasts some beautiful old buildings and I hoped to find sustenance in a homely tea-room packed with floral china and chintz. There was such a place – hurrah! So a pile of jam-and-cream scones were devoured in less than 40 minutes. Settling back into the ute, I adjusted my waistband. Clumsily the car departed town with a squeal and cloud of dust.

A signpost for Launceston brought a smug sense of satisfaction – I'd somehow managed to navigate a lolloping vehicle all the way from Hobart to the South Esk River. I patted the ute, grabbed my bag, found a garden cafe and a glass of one of Tasmania's delectable home-spun wines. The curious Tasmanian devil had eluded me, but I had encountered the magic of the Earth's last great temperate wilderness. In a ute.

Contacts:
Tasmania Tourist Board
www.discovertasmania.com.au

CENTRAL ARNHEM HIGHWAY, AUSTRALIA

In the Australian Outback, far up in the Northern Territory, the road from Katherine to Gove (also known as Nhulunbuy) denotes the point where the Gulf of Carpentaria meets the Arafura Sea. In such remote lands there is the thrill of survival: the human body requires a high water intake in 35°C heat – the average Aboriginal male can drink three-and-a-half litres in 35 seconds. But it isn't just the driver on a road-trip that needs liquid; cars also need fuel and water to keep them rolling along. On this unsealed, dusty 710-kilometre (441-mile) stretch there is a single, solitary petrol station. Otherwise it is a route of glorious isolation. Mysterious and magical, with deep bright colours in its landscape, the Central Arnhem Highway is also a place of sacred meaning and is depicted in Aboriginal art. Cross two major rivers, meet the indigenous community in Maningrida and be wowed by some of the most extraordinary wildlife in the world before you reach mainland Northern Territory's far north-eastern tip and the lush, green town of Gove.

When you know there is just one fuel stop on a mammoth road-trip across hot, harsh terrain, it is hard not to be haunted by worry. Using a non-scientific calculation to tally the number of jerrycans I needed didn't help – but how else to allow for unforeseen headwinds and unexpected detours? One thing is certain, you need a 4×4 vehicle as the route is rough and rugged, with two rivers and several creeks to cross. Permits (free) are required to cross clan lands: get these from the Northern Land Council.

This trip stretches from Katherine, about 320 kilometres (199 miles) south-east of Darwin, in the Northern Territory's north-east through Arnhem Land, the Parsons and Mitchell Ranges to Nhulunbuy on the Gulf of Carpentaria. The area has been the home of Aboriginal people for thousands and thousands of years and was first discovered by the Dutch in the early 1600s. This is one of Australia's remote but beautiful areas: a wilderness that offers incredible countryside and impressive amounts of Aboriginal culture. During the Second World War, the Gove peninsula played a vital role in Australia's defences against attacks from the north. The region was named after a British airman called Gove who was killed there. It has been a place of considerable struggle and resentment since the 1970s, when bauxite mining began in the area without any consultation with the local Aboriginal people. It caused great displeasure and eventually led to the Northern Territory Land Rights Act in the mid-1970s, which effectively handed the region back to its traditional owners. Since then, there has been a greater respect for indigenous peoples and their beliefs, tradition, art and cultures.

From Katherine to Bulman, the first place you hit is Beswick (also known as Wugularr), a little over 60 kilometres (37 miles) from the Stuart Highway turn-off. It's a bumpy, dusty road from here to the Mainoru Store where you can camp, get provisions and fuel up before Nhulunbuy (though rumour has it, there's an emergency supply at Bulman 70 kilometres/44 miles on). If you're an angling enthusiast, take a look at the Mainoru River: the waters are so rich in fish the locals say they jump out and flip into the net.

Once you've passed through Bulman, the first major obstacle comes into view – the Wilton River. Conditions

Photo: CSIRO

vary here, and travel reports can be misleading. On the day I crossed it, the depth was about a foot all the way across on the right-hand side – but the middle was much, much deeper. Fed by nine creeks and rivers, the Wilton starts at an elevation of 283 metres (928 feet) and ends near Wilton Crossing at an elevation of 7.7 metres (just over 25 feet), merging with the Roper River. It is important to stop, get out of your vehicle and observe the Wilton for a while – it is renowned for catching people out on this crossing. Look out for saltwater crocodiles, 'salties', which inhabit this river; the most aggressive species, their formidable jaws can snap bones like twigs. These ferocious hunters are opportunistic predators, so any animal, in or out of the water, is fair game. So stay at least 3 metres from the water's edge. Don't assume just because you can't see a crocodile one isn't there; they can stay under water for over an hour.

The soft dirt on the roughshod track improves a little as you motor towards Emu Springs and the dust haze starts to clear. This campsite has zero facilities but is conveniently located just off the road. From here, approximately 30 kilometres (19 miles) along the road, the next hazard awaits. As a rule of thumb, the locals swear that the Goyder River is usually twice as troublesome to cross as the Wilton River, so take extra special care. Spend time looking around before deciding on the best crossing point, which may not be the obvious one. As at the Wilton River, watch out for salties.

From here you will leave the Mitchell Range behind and begin entering the Frederick Hills, about 580 kilometres (360 miles) east of Darwin. A road turning south heads through the Bath Range, to Jalma Bay, Blue Mud Bay and, ultimately, Numbulwar, which is situated on the western side of the Gulf of Carpentaria, a distinctive rectangular shape that indents Australia's northern coast. Along this dusty road, with Gove around 240 kilometres (149 miles) away, it is strange to spot a concrete table and chairs set by a roadside creek.

Not far up the road is the turn-off to Lake Evella, the home of a Gapuwiyak community, about 500 kilometres (310 miles) east of Darwin and 120 kilometres (75 miles) west of Nhulunbuy. Aboriginal people have inhabited this region for 40,000 years and on the shores of Lake Evella is one of the Northern Territory's easternmost settlements. Methodist missionaries established the Gapuwiyak community in the 1960s to supply timber for missions in the region. Workers came from the surrounding areas of Burrum, Raymangirr, Bunhanura and Balma, and from Galiwin'ku. In the 1970s the mission ended and Gapuwiyak became Aboriginal land under the Aboriginal Land Rights (Northern Territory) Act 1976. Today the population of Gapuwiyak and its surrounds is approximately 874, of which 824 are indigenous (94 per cent). About 40 per cent of Gapuwiyak's indigenous population are younger than twenty. They speak Djambarrpuyngu (a dialect of Yolngu Matha) in the main (76 per cent) with the rest speaking Ritharrngu and Dhalwangu. The population is predominantly Yolngu, with people from eleven different Yolngu groups.

It's a smoother run for the last 200 kilometres (124 miles) on the approach to Nhulunbuy, flanked by tall woodlands and with several crossings over small rocky creeks. On the final stretch, the dust turns to asphalt, signifying that Nhulunbuy is nearing – a sign eventually tells you that you've reached the northern end of the Gove Peninsula, but your eyes have already widened at the sight of the seductive waters of the pristine Arafura Sea.

As a dirt road, the Central Arnhem Highway is susceptible to wind, rain and harsh heat. Be particularly careful at night – buffaloes and other animals can stray on to the road.

Do not speed. Carry a decent kit box with tools, puncture repair equipment, jack, spare tyres, blankets, torch and food. If a road has been closed, do not attempt to travel on it. Be careful crossing flooded roads or bridges unless you can be absolutely certain of the depth of water. Watch out for saltwater crocodiles. Permits to cross aboriginal land aren't given to caravans, camper vans, motorbikes or anyone carrying firearms or alcohol.

Contacts:
Australian Tourist Board
www.visitaustralia.com

NEW ZEALAND'S SOUTH ISLAND

To travel New Zealand's South Island is to see different countries' landscapes in one place, from towering Alpine mountains and Scottish heathland one moment to the golden sandy beaches of the Mediterranean, France's picture-perfect vineyards and Iceland's thermal hot springs. Driving South Island in a set time frame is no easy task because there is simply so darn much to see. The landscape just induces gushing hyperbole at every turn. I began to bore myself, repeating the words awesome, wow, great, incredible, stunning, fantastic and gorgeous – but try as I might, I couldn't stop.

Most big road tours of South Island begin in Christchurch as this is where most international airlines fly to. The charming historic core of this city has been twice devastated by earthquake in recent years. There are huge gaps where buildings once stood. Other buildings are undergoing painstaking restoration, with every part of the community involved in some way. Pick up a rental car from the airport, or if you want something quirkier book it in Christchurch – they have the usual dented mechanical misfits to choose from for half the price of a flashier motor. Me, I opted for a well-used camper van, poorly painted in the colour of avocado. With dints, scrapes and signs of rust, it was clearly an elderly Queen of the Road, yet when I started her, the engine sounded as smooth as Manuka honey. I let it run, enjoying the gentle, low pitch of the rat-rat-rat. Who knew that the sound of massive quantities of rapidly oxidising fossil fuel could sound so good?

New Zealand is full of people road-tripping in camper vans; the etiquette is to wave at any you pass. As a self-contained unit, it makes overnighting a breeze – you can pull up at any campground. Before you push your pedal to the floor, visit the Sign of the Kiwi – arguably the most panoramic of Christchurch's viewpoints as it encapsulates a vast swathe of the most beautiful part of the city. Cool organic cafes, juice bars and restaurants that are quietly buzzing make Christchurch a nice place to hang out. If you can, grab a seat at one of the pavement joints around the city centre – sunny weather brings people out on to the streets and it's great to watch the world go by.

From the wine bars of Christchurch you head north up through the leafy wine-growing region of Canterbury. Here, where the cool foothills of the Southern Alps tumble down to meet New Zealand's most extensive lowlands, a whole host of celebrated wine producers craft outstanding Pinot Noir, Riesling and Chardonnay – and much more. This most exciting of New Zealand's wine regions is just a leisurely 40-minute drive from Christchurch. Many of the top wineries

Photo: Achim

offer vineyard tours and cellar door tastings that are suitable for plonk guzzlers and connoisseurs alike.

After the coastal town of Cheviot, it is full steam ahead to Kaikoura further up on the picturesque east coast (around 200 kilometres/124 miles from Christchurch). This particularly attractive rural seaside town sits perched on a rocky peninsula, protruding from lush farmland beneath the mountains. The surrounding waters boast a complex marine system that provides an abundantly rich habitat for marine mammals and seabirds. Whales, seals, albatross and dolphins thrive here – in fact over seventeen species of whale are found within 8 kilometres of the coastline. Numerous ecologically sound whale-watching tours run from Kaikoura, which last for about three hours. I felt a strange gurgling in the pit of my stomach as the boat rolled with the swells out to sea – not seasickness, but high excitement as I scrutinised the waters! We bounced atop the chop once well offshore, and sea-spray drenched us all to the skin. With wind-weathered ropes and tarpaulins flapping and dials bleeping, the boat surged on full-throttle before lurching to a sudden halt. Bobbin in hypnotic silence, a deafening whoosh filled the air and the waters parted, sending seabirds high into the sky. A vast black shadow revealed itself with a 'boom' as it pounded the water with a mighty swish of its hefty black tail. I almost wept with joy. A glistening arched back, a dorsal fin, a large eye, a peaked snout and a graceful dive into the deep: in a split second, the king of the ocean is gone, leaving only a towering spume of misty water in its wake. Wow, oh wow. Few superlatives can match the moment. You can spot whales any time of year at Kaikoura: most trips have a 95 per cent success rate.

The camper van and I enjoyed an early morning meander along winding roads into the Southern Alps, where I took a dip in the thermal waters at Hanmer Springs. Next stop Hokitika, reached by a mountain pass that crosses to the South Island's west coast: a peaceful piece of paradise with few cars and a striking coastline strewn with rocks the size of double-decker buses. From here it's a 140-kilometre (87-mile) trip south to the Franz Josef Glacier through the most extraordinary mix of terrain: first rainforest, then coast, beach and mountains. Take a guided ice walk or a helicopter flight to the top of the glacier for a long soak in bubbling geo-thermal pools.

The 280-kilometre (174-mile) route from Franz Josef Glacier to Wanaka ranks among the prettiest and most dramatic in New Zealand, as it takes you over the magnificent Haast Pass. The flora-rich scenery here compels you to lock up the car and walk, touch and smell the wild flowers – resistance is futile. Leave plenty of time for taking photos as there are umpteen spectacular waterfalls.

From the blissful shores of Lake Wanaka, it's a relatively short 90-minute jaunt to the rugged extremes of Queenstown, so there is plenty of time to take a kayak out for a paddle among brightly coloured birds and butterflies. Loads of deep canyoning trips also depart from here: I tried the Leaping Burn Max – which is every bit as manic as it sounds! First you leap 10 metres into the water, before a lot of scrambling over rocks and climbing. Then it's lots of abseiling down cliffs – tough but utterly exhilarating – with a 14-metre jump into a deep pool as a madcap finale! After this, I felt ready for Queenstown: the 'The Adventure Capital of the World'. But if you're happy to give skydiving, bungie-jumping, paragliding and white-water rafting a miss, there's a more relaxed way to sightsee Queenstown: from Lake Wakatipu on a 1912 vintage twin-screw steam ship, the TSS *Earnslaw*.

It may be a five-hour drive to Mt Cook from Queenstown but every kilometre is utterly spectacular. Look out for roadside stalls selling Manuka honey, fresh fruit ice cream, flowers and lots of wonderful cheeses. Cross the Lindis Pass into Mackenzie Country, a region famous for its cotton-wool-soft Merino sheep and wool industry, before arriving at Lake Tekapo and its turquoise-coloured waters. Make sure you are at Lake Tekapo for sunset: it would be a crime to miss witnessing the sky turn crimson, pink and gold. If the weather is clear during your visit, book a one-hour sightseeing flight that skirts around the peaks of Mount Cook – the views are unbeatable across the valleys and you'll feel on top of the world.

Contacts:
New Zealand Tourist Board
www.newzealand.com

ASIA AND THE MIDDLE EAST

OVERWATER HIGHWAY, CHINA

On a particularly curvaceous stretch of coastline in Central China, the Overwater Highway drew crowds of spectators when it opened in 2014. People came from hundreds of miles around to see this revolutionary road-bridge for themselves. Rumours had circulated for years about a route that would allow drivers to, literally, drive over water, but few believed them. So it was a special day for Central China, and the 11-kilometre (6.8-mile) Overwater Highway didn't disappoint: it is in a beautiful river valley with its gasp-inducing views. Designed with top eco-credentials, the road follows the shape of the landscape to link Xingshan County in mountainous Hubei to the G42 high-speed route that connects Shanghai in eastern China to Chengdu in the south-west. Considerable care was taken not to disturb the abundance of plants and woodlands in the mountains, with every bit of manpower provided by local villagers – an incredible feat.

Rural China can be a tricky place in which to travel with its poorly funded road maintenance and limited infrastructure. While Beijing and Shanghai roads are built, repaired and tended with vast budgets and slavish devotion, travel out into the sticks and the asphalt soon crumbles into nothing but dust. In the decade since cars became available to the ordinary man, accidents have become common and fatalities are soaring. Roads are busy: cars have increased by 15 million each year since 2001 and each year around 50,000 people die on the road – a staggering annual tally. Around two-thirds of the road sits on top of an elevated bridge that runs along the middle of a river valley, slicing travel time from Xingshan to the Yiba Expressway to just twenty minutes and avoiding a steep and convoluted road. It splits into two as it meets a mountain along the route, a design chosen specifically to avoid damage to the mountain's ecology. It's a sympathetic construction, built in harmony with the landscape – a $70-million project that has been dubbed 'the most beautiful overwater highway'.

In a car, we travelled alongside the entire length of the river, hugging the outer edges of the slopes. Fellow users of the highway appeared to be a mix of commuters and truck

Photo: Rex/Shutterstock

drivers – though it has become a popular tourist attraction as a first-of-its-kind. Now villagers living in the most remote mountain villages can interact with the towns and bigger cities that were once so out of reach. Like me they seemed elated to be crossing the series of towering concrete-and-steel columns of the viaduct – the S-shaped curves: long, winding, exciting and sensuous.

Road-tripping this highway offers a chance to explore the mountainous Hubei region: an area rich in the most ancient of Chinese cultures. Located in the middle reaches of the Yangtze River, to the north of Dongting Lake, Hubei Province is bordered by Henan Province to the north, Anhui to the east, Jiangxi to the south-east, Hunan to the south, Sichuan to the west and Shaanxi to the north-west. It covers around 180,000 square kilometres (about 69,500 square miles) and has a large population of more than 60 million. The capital city, Wuhan, is the economic powerhouse of the province's south-east. China considers Hubei to be one of the originating places of the Chinese people and its early civilisations. It is home to numerous minority ethnic groups, including Miao, Tujia and Dong together with a riot of colourful festivals, song and traditional dance theatre. The long history of the Hubei region ensures it is richly endowed with ancient towers, grottoes, archaeological remains and imperial mausoleums and temples. Wudang Mountain, a sacred Taoist peak dotted with hundreds of temples and palaces, is deeply rooted in local culture. East Lake, located on the eastern side of Wuchang City, is the biggest lake within a city in China. The world-famous Yangtze Three Gorges Dam Project – China's largest water conservation project – is close to Yichang City and is a spectacular sight of crashing, steep water cascades set within lush, green mountain slopes.

The Overwater Highway brings the neon-lit shopping

districts, restaurants and expat watering holes of the financial hub Shanghai closer to the mountain folk of Hubei. This sprawling metropolis is a dazzling mix of needle-thin high-rise buildings housing the most influential names in global trade and the bird-filled estuary of the Yangtze River, and it is this unusual blend of the sophisticated and simple that gives Shanghai its glamour. Old and new, modern and traditional, western and oriental all meet here – with Shanghai Disney (due to open in summer 2016) and Parisian boulevard shopping and the charming backstreets of the old, walled Nanshi District examples of the city's extremes.

Renowned for its fine, spicy traditional cuisine throughout the whole of China, Chengdu is the capital of Sichuan Province, where the peppercorn of the same name peps up almost every dish. The city is situated in an area with an abundance of mineral resources and on extremely fertile land. Crops benefit from a super-slick transport system that whizzes fresh produce from the hinterland of China across the country by air, road and railway. I followed the example of other road-trippers and grabbed a table in a kerb-side teahouse and sipped on delicate white tea while watching the people of Chengdu go by. The history of the city can be traced back 2,400 years, when the first emperor built his capital. The city still bears its original name and is packed with amazing bronze statues – an indispensable part of ancient Chinese culture. From my seat on the busy thoroughfare, I watched an old man practising the ancient art of calligraphy, with a caged songbird by his side, while women sorted dried fish into buckets and children chased petals fluttering in the breeze. So after toasting China's first over-the-water highway with gin-clear tea, I bought a carton of salty rice noodles from a street vendor and ate them while reminiscing about the magnificent valley. I recalled the

Highway and the wide, expansive panoramas of mountain, water and sky that it reveals.

Just one tip for this road-trip: make the most of this route, don't rush – don't even blink! It may have taken years to build, but it'll take just minutes to drive it, so be sure to soak it all up.

Contacts:
China Tourist Board
www.cnto.org

VIETNAM'S NORTHERN LOOP

This elongated route through mist-topped purple mountains, cattle-filled paths, verdant jungle and thatched villages buzzing with chickens, rice markets and bicycles has been dubbed the 'ultimate Asian road-trip' – and rightly so. Vehicles are few and far between on the legendary North-West Loop and the scenery is unforgettable, providing a fascinating glimpse into Vietnam's less-visited rural backroads through rice terraces, karst formations and thundering waterfalls.

Begin in the city of Hanoi. Use a 4WD, if you can, because mountain roads are often scattered with rocks and debris. Like all the best road-trips, you'll use both the air-conditioner and the heater in the same day. Straight stretches of sealed asphalt can turn into twisty, tight coils of rough dirt built in an era before the motor car. In Vietnam, the preferred mode of transport is a 125cc semi-automatic 'moto-scooter' and wherever you are you'll see swarms of them buzzing about like demented flies. They even chance their luck on the hellish highway (H6) that shoots out of the centre of

Photo: Jaybeetkamay

Hanoi. It takes just half an hour of maniacal truck drivers swinging their trailers from one lane to another and loud, blasting horns, but by the time you've reached the turn-off it feels as if you've aged a decade or more. Unclamp your fingers from the wheel, wipe your brow and breathe. Never again will you complain about traffic back home.

The skinny two-lane secondary road weaves its way through rice terraces on an alternative route to Mai Chau. From here continue on to the ethnically diverse Son La: no more than a regional transport hub but home to Vietnam's White Thai, Black Thai, Meo and Muong ethnic minorities. Until the 20th century, Vietnamese influence was minimal, so the area around the city has a unique character. It is also beautiful, with the suburbs fanning out into impressive, lush surrounding countryside. Apart from gurgling irrigation pumps and rustling palms, and an occasional squawk or crow, the simple villages are quiet. Take the lush valley roads that twist and turn up to the mountains – every one of the dozen or so peaks in view is a different shade of vibrant green.

From Son La, head to Dien Bien Phu (known as 'DBP') on the QL279 turn-off to stroll the land where one of the biggest game-changing military victories in modern history took place. French defeat here in 1954 signalled the end of French influence in Indochina and the battle fought at DBP was the last major campaign by a European state in the region. The loss of life was colossal; a walk around Hill A-1 and the war cemetery's unmarked graves provides a grim insight into the region's war-torn past.

Next it is time to head into Sapa, the busy centre of northern Vietnam where some evidence of French influence remains. As a strategic former French hill station, the town boasts astonishing far-reaching views over a misty valley of waterfalls and rice paddies. Today it is famous for the adventure sports that take place in many of its most beautiful locations, such as mountain biking blue-tinged mountain passes and trekking long paths to meet the local Hmong hill tribes. Sapa is also a nice place to overnight during the Northern Loop road-trip, or you could head east to stay in a stilt-house in Pac Ngoi village, among bears, tigers and king cobra, on the shores of Ba Be Lake. As Vietnam's largest natural body of water, Ba Be Lake provides a majestic centrepiece set amid limestone, waterfalls, caves and unusual rock formations. A designated UNESCO World Heritage Site, Ba Be National Park is richly forested with wooden huts built up high to offer overnight guests jaw-dropping sweeping views across the tree tops and beyond.

As Vietnam's northern-most province, Ha Giang has a mysterious landscape along the Chinese border: a strange topography of conical limestone peaks and deep, craterous valleys cut with roaring rivers. Though it suffers from a reputation as a scruffy, lawless frontier town, Ha Giang City offers passers-through a certain charm. Set aside the Lo (Blue) River, which despite its name runs brown like a frothy cappuccino, it has a bustling centre strung with steam-filled rice eateries (*quán cơm*). From here, below forested limestone mountains, is a weaving road to the Dong Van Karst Plateau Geo-Park: a giant Hollywood-style sign set into the hillside (conveniently in Vietnamese and English) points the way.

Next, a long snaking ascent leads to a pass crossing over a treeless plateau, after which the road falls sharply into a valley. At the end of a series of severe switchbacks, the road crosses a deep canyon into a bamboo-lined stretch alongside a muddy boulder-strewn river where children play. The road rises and falls at strangely rhythmic intervals, creating a fluid dreamlike sensation. Isolated villages hidden deep in the rocks have planted crops of soy, pumpkins and rice along the roadside. On lower slopes, you'll find rice fields, maize fields and stands of bamboo where opium poppies once thrived. Peasants rest on boulders, their backs piled high with heavy loads of wood. There are deep basins with the acoustics of an amphitheatre: send your car into a skid here and the chilling sound of screeching tyres will echo for miles. Drive Vietnam's Northern Loop, if you can, when the road is dry and the weather warm (spring and autumn) – the colours along this stretch are bright and rainfall is light, though your average speed will still be less than 30 kilometres an hour.

Contacts:
Vietnam Tourist Board
www.vietnamtourism.com

GOBI DESERT, MONGOLIA

Road-tripping the Gobi Desert is a daunting proposition, for it covers an immense expanse of land. Roads are scarce and hire vehicles limited – you'll likely end up in a Russian minivan with zero suspension. In gritty, arid conditions, you'll need to be prepared for long days being flung about in your seat like a sock in a tumble-drier. Sand storms can make visibility negligible and there is nothing more frustrating than knowing that views of sand dunes, gorges, cliffs and caves are all out there, somewhere beyond the eye-stinging blizzard of sand. There will be periods when you feel you're wasting time in an airless vehicle driving aimlessly over samey ground for miles and miles and miles. Then there will be the moments when the Gobi Desert sends a sensory jolt through your entire body: a reminder, should you need one, that it is one of the most fantastic landscapes on Earth.

So, despite the risks of bad weather and sunrise-to-sunset drives, it's a great place to visit. Why? Well, for a start few expanses are as rich in history and colour as the fossil-ridden Gobi Desert. There is also the added attraction of the 'singing sands' of the Khongoryn Els region, where the chorus emitted by the rounded grains as the winds pass across the dunes adds to the other-worldly character of these lands. Extending 185 kilometres (115 miles) across the southern Gobi between Mounts Sevrei and Zuulun, this vast, empty space boasts incredible paleontological riches together with scatterings of wooded tufts of elm. Peaks soar up to over 76 metres (250 feet) with the Hongoriin Gol River at the northern edge of the dunes a gathering point for the animal species of the region. As he forged his vast empire in the 13th century, warrior Genghis Khan and his soldiers once galloped across the golden steppes amid oases, wild sheep, gazelles and an abundance of birds.

The sand's musical repertoire ranges from a gentle low, deep hum to a high-pitched 'operatic-style' shriek and crescendo-roar, with the outer layer of undulating dunes acting as a giant amplifier. Songs can last for a few seconds, or can continue for minutes if not hours. If you can, broker an arrangement with a local community to spend time with a local family – it's easy enough to secure an invitation to a traditional ger (Mongolian yurt) and it is fascinating to witness the age-old customs of the Gobi's nomadic people first hand. Ulan Bator-based community tour company Ger to Ger gives back to the families who host – it works hard to maintain a sustainable relationship between tourists and local families and prides itself on genuine, authentic encounters in which the smallest communities benefit long term.

Photo: Arabsalam

After spending a day in Ulan Bator, the madcap Mongolian capital city, I acquainted myself with an elderly minivan of no distinguishable brand and readied myself for the great outdoors. With my boots, scarf and sunblock stripes, I looked like a desert junkie – and I was excited at the prospect of discovering one as diverse as the Gobi. Once bags and bodies were loaded into the van, we edged our way out of gridlocked traffic and out into the open steppe. Within minutes the rolling green hillside caught my breath as we left the crazy jams and blaring horns of the city behind and bumped through the countryside – a bone-rattling, joint-jarring journey.

A whole twelve hours later, we arrived at the ger. Our guide passed around a sharp-tasting liquor 'to kill any bacteria in our stomachs' and we all duly took a swig. To the comforting snuffles and snores of the family and its livestock, already deep in early slumber, we yawned wide and deep while watching the sun set over the sands. Rolled up in a blanket that smelt of goat, I rubbed my bruised and battered limbs: despite uncomfortable travelling, my spirits were high and I fell asleep wondering what tomorrow would bring.

We stirred early next morning to the persistent sounds of goats and sheep, with smiling children peering inside our ger. After a breakfast of bread as hard as stone washed down with warm horse's milk, we packed up our things and studied a weird-looking rock, stooping against the fierce winds. After saying our goodbyes, and leaving small gifts of crayons and colouring books for the kids, we headed off towards Flaming Cliffs, the famous site where dinosaur eggs were first discovered in 1922. In the early sun, the spotlight was perfectly placed: the cliff-tops glowed ruby-red licked by a flickering backdrop of yellow-orange. Back on the road, the van slid around on a shifting sand trail before hitting sun-baked hard mud. We lost well over an hour in an encounter with a herd of camels blocking the road: wild desert camels are grumpy two-humped beasts with a hatred of humans.

Later that day, once we'd arrived at our ger, we took the chance to ride one of the domesticated camels, bareback. At all times, it was the camel, not me, who was captain, pilot and navigator – but honestly, after eight hours at the wheel it felt good to relinquish control and simply cling on for the ride. Apart from the bony-backed camel's uncomfortable rolling gait. Plus I had the smell of camel up my nose for hours afterwards, and itching legs where its fleas had nibbled.

Next day was another bumpy eight-hour stint – with a half-hour stop for lunch at a truly beautiful gorge. Wild wolves and birds call this place home. I gazed down on to passing herds of horses after we prepared to overnight at a ger camp, set in a stunning location on rolling steppe hills. Dinner included deep bowls of homemade beef noodle broth and lamb-stuffed pancake (*khuushuur*) – delicious, wholesome and filling. I pinched myself: I'm in the company of ger-dwelling nomads among the ghost of Genghis Khan and shimmering distant oases.

There was slightly less driving the next day: just seven-and-a-half hours – but the seat in the van had practically moulded itself to my backside by then. The journey became more interesting; the rolling hills scenery slowly transformed back into the flat, dusty desert. The views of the sands in the changing light had a mesmerising effect. We also came across human life, rather than just a glimpse of an occasional desert fox, ibex or bird of prey. A family with ten children was stiffening sheep wool by dragging it along behind a camel in the dust: once the wool has been rolled for several miles, it becomes like matted candy floss and is used, like felt, to line and insulate the inside of a ger.

The noise of an approaching storm was louder than a

steam train and amplified by the mountains that surrounded us. Wrapping our scarves tightly around our faces, we narrowed our eyes. Gobi winds are the strongest I have ever encountered – there is nothing to do but dig your heels in hard because strong gusts carry vast clouds of sand in wave-like ripples. A few spindly shrubs and trees act as a windbreak to take the brunt of the wind's force. Before our eyes, the road disappeared and all tread marks and tracks were wiped out by the storm. Everything about our immediate location had been altered dramatically, beyond recognition. To become so disorientated in just a few minutes is terrifying: an authentic Gobi experience if ever there was one.

The desert isn't featureless or empty, though it may take a while for your eyes to adjust to the terrain. Around 200 million years ago the Gobi was a vast inland sea. After the ocean came the dinosaurs. Today ibex, argali (wild sheep) and pika (a rabbit-sized rodent) are the main residents as well as the bearded vulture and golden eagle. You may even see larks, cranes and sand grouse in the ever-changing light.

Driving yourself in the Gobi desert is only advisable if you hire a guide to join your group of family and friends. I preferred this to an organised tour because it still felt like an independent road trip. I wanted the freedom to make spontaneous detours.

So what to pack? Wet wipes are invaluable (there are no showers in the Gobi), bug spray essential (there are lots of flies and mosquitoes) and a hat and sunscreen crucial (for obvious reasons). I also packed a light shawl, which I wrapped around my head to cover my nose and mouth when driving through heavy sand and dust. Brace yourself for extremely rustic outhouse (long-drop) style toilets – not the worst I've seen by a long margin but it's a lesson in body posture and balance nonetheless. Unless you find fermented camel's milk refreshing, you can never have enough water (or toilet paper). Body spray is sensible too, as being around goat, sheep and camels soon takes its toll.

Contacts:
Mongolia Tourist Board
www.visitmongolia.com

TAIHANG MOUNTAINS, CHINA

China's Taihang Mountain Range runs 250 miles from north to south through Shanxi, Henan and Hebei Provinces. Peaks soar from 1,524 metres (5,000 feet) to 1,981 metres (6,500 feet) with the principal peak of Xiao Wutaishan soaring up to a staggering 2,882 metres (9,455 feet). Deep in the Taihang Mountains, a scattering of teeny-weeny villages lie hidden in plunging valleys. In China the mountains are a national treasure and much-climbed now since the installation of a 91-metre (300-foot) spiral staircase dubbed the 'Stairway to Heaven'. It's no easily climbed staircase – you need to be fit, not suffer from vertigo, be aged under 60 and have no heart or lung problems. Me, I prefer the thrill of driving the mighty Taihang Mountains' Guoliang Tunnel road that also scales the towering peaks: this incredible feat of construction was dug entirely by hand, which is almost incomprehensible. For centuries the remote mountain settlement of Guoliang was totally cut off from the outside world. When the Chinese Government refused funding for a tunnel road, the locals took matters into their own hands, hacking a hole through the rock with picks and shovels in order to be connected to the rest of China. It took thirteen villagers five years to

Photo: FANG Chen

finish the 1,200-metre (3,937-foot) tunnel road – the result is a 5-metre (16-foot) high by 4-metre (13-foot) wide route that can (just) accommodate two passing vehicles. Rustic dungeon-like gashes, now used as windows, form oddly shaped spy-holes high up over the valley. They were carved in the rocks to make it easier for the workers to push the rubble out. For the untrained labour-force, the construction of the tunnel proved highly dangerous as it required extensive use of explosives on some of China's steepest cliffs. Although two men died in accidents, the others resolved to keep on digging. It took 4,000 hammers, 12 tons of steel and hundreds and hundreds of chisels – bought with the proceeds of selling goats and herbs. But after more than 1,800 days, on 1 May 1977 the tunnel was joyously opened to traffic.

Around the tunnel, the surrounding mountains are large and imposing so that vehicles look like tiny ants. It looks unworldly: in truth, the Taihang Mountains are unlike anywhere else on Earth.

When you drive the tunnel it is impossible not to feel the spirit of human endeavour: every rough-hewn furrow, cut, gouge and chisel mark tells the tale of blood, sweat and tears. Without proper equipment, the men relied on primitive handmade tools. The craftsmanship is awe-inspiring. Study the road surface ahead or pass your hand over the tunnel walls to sense the backbreaking chipping away at impenetrable rock: the scale of it is overwhelming. Today the Guoliang Tunnel has become a tourist attraction known throughout China: everyone who visits is astounded that it is the work of just thirteen men.

To reach Guoliang, and its tricky-to-find tunnel roads, start your trip in Xinxiang, a city in Henan Province. Head north from here on Huanyu Avenue (otherwise known as the S229). After 21 kilometres (13 miles) you'll hit the town of Huixian and another stretch of the S229. After about 21 kilometres (15 miles) you'll reach a junction with the S228: turn left here and keep following the S229 past water-logged rice paddies for another 13 kilometres (8 miles). When you reach the village of Nanzhaizen, you'll see a sign for Guoliang – turn left and it's about 15 kilometres (9 miles) further until the entrance of the tunnel.

Be warned: the tunnel is used by foot passengers (often large family groups) and animals (goats generally) as well as vehicles (anything from a tricycle towing a cart to a truck). Uneven walls, and a road with some serious gradients, ensure that the Guoliang Tunnel is ranked as one of the top ten steepest routes in the world. It is perilous in wet conditions: slippery and prone to dramatic skids. Piles of crushed rocks lie in the foothills thousands of feet below the tunnel – and no car wants to join them. It takes the careful balancing of velocity with momentum, together with smooth application of brakes. Gear-crunching is inevitable on the dogleg zigzags and plumes of grit can hamper vision on the dust-busting ascent. Small stone turrets, no bigger than plant pots, line the edges of the S-curves and claim to provide some measure of safety – though I'm certain it is mainly psychological. Belching lorries thunder past, surging power at every curb-hugging spur. I leant into the bend, involuntarily, my hand tight around the gear lever for some quick-shifting action on the turn. I was terrified I'd lose propulsion and roll backwards into free-fall, yet felt equally anxious of pushing the pedal to the metal: excess pressure could shoot the car over the precipice. However, incomparable views made the stress worthwhile.

Once you've reached the end of the tunnel, consider stretching your legs and venturing into a truly unique landscape: hiking to one of the two neighbouring villages,

Kunshan and Xiyagou. A 2-mile trail boasted some eye-popping views across valleys and mountain tops – it felt like you could reach out and grab a handful of cloud. To do it by car, make the 89-kilometre (55-mile) journey through the Taihang Mountains: a scenic tour that takes you along deeply rutted secret roads flanked by scrubby plateaus neatly divided by rice terraces and aromatic herb gardens. Weaving in and out of tiny bamboo villages, the route eventually delivers you into a chaos of farm-track congestion. Once you've negotiated herds of buffalo, flapping chickens and a flotilla of vintage ploughs, it is time to take a slip road tunnel that leads to a tree-topped summit with top-dollar panoramas across Xiyagou.

Contacts:
China Tourist Board
www.cnto.org

LEH–MANALI HIGHWAY, INDIA

Progress is slow on India's Leh–Manali Highway: a 480-kilometre (298-mile) Himalayan mountain pass isolated from civilisation by more than 4,000 metres (13,123 feet). Moving inches at a time, I was wedged between two wheezing trucks in a crocodile of vehicles. We were nose-to-bumper, jolting and jarring, on a treacherously narrow ledge. Small ragged rocks – dislodged by the heavy, staccato braking – fell on to the roof of my Mahindra Maxximo Mini Van. Bouncing off, they left sharp dints in the paintwork. Ping. Pong. Ding. Each one ricocheted at tangents before being silently swallowed by the chasm. Meanwhile, I – and several hundred tons of whining metal before and behind me – was praying that our knife-edge precipice was more solid than it felt. Following a zigzag route that stretches across Northern India, from Leh in Ladakh state to Manali in the state of Himachal Pradesh, the Highway is one of the world's highest mountain passes in the world. Uncertain weather, a dizzying lack of oxygen, dirt tracks, isolation and biting cold soon take their toll on those who drive this road. As well as extra fuel, I carried a tangle of lucky talismans: I felt closer to heaven in more ways than one.

Typically, the journey from Manali to Leh is attempted as a full day's slog, morning-to-night. Schedules are meaningless on this unruly stretch because renegade wildlife, spontaneous downpours and clapped-out motors often cause delay. Officially open only in the summer months, the Leh–Manali Highway's highest elevations tip more than 5,328 metres (17,480 feet) at the Taglang La mountain pass. Situated in the Ladakh region of the Indian state of Jammu and Kashmir, this Buddhist-prayer-flag-strewn section is partially paved but reached by a steep 20-kilometre (12-mile) loose-stone climb that soars 700 metres (2,297 feet) and offers zero traction. A local sign at the summit incorrectly states you've reached 5,359 metres – and it is tempting to quibble with an inanimate object when altitude sickness has sapped all your strength.

The queue I was in was several miles long and formed of a broad mix of vehicles, from sales men in mid-range saloons, rusty motorbikes and construction trucks to school minibuses and delivery vans carrying everything from rolls of sari fabric to big silver vats of *ghee* (Indian butter). In winter, as fast as the snow is cleared, avalanches block the road again. Heavy snowfalls and patches of ice bring extreme danger. Road closures are frequent. Yet the road is

Photo: Ashoosaini2002

driven year-round, cutting through snow-capped mountains and over white-topped snaking stretches. The Indian army patches up this road when the potholes get as big as a 7.5 ton Isuzu truck (Ladakh, wedged between China and Pakistan, is important in strategic terms for India). Peer down to the lower slopes and you can see the twisted wreckage of vehicles that haven't made it: uncertain terrain requires skill and patience.

Set within the Beas River Valley, sandwiched among towering peaks, the start of the road at Manali looks out across fruit orchards and rocky streams. But the first amazing views are of Rohtang Pass, 50 kilometres (31 miles) from the centre of the city, where expansive panoramas take in blue-white glaciers and the ski slopes of Snow Point. Grand mountain and valley views abound in beautiful Keylong in lush, green Bhaga Valley close to the monasteries Shasur and Gemur. Set by the Chandra River, the small village of Jispa is looped by trickling streams and lush woodlands with trails to 10,000 feet (3,048 metres) above sea level and gorgeous far-reaching views. Trekking trails riddle the rocky peaks around the traditional Himalayan village of Darcha, located beside the Bhaga River, around 35 kilometres (22 miles) from Keylong. This is where climbers pick up the popular Darcha–Padum trail, a scenic 9–10 days' trek.

Between Jispa and Sarchu, you'll find the local watering hole the Zingzing Bar, which boasts the distinction of being one of the highest roadside bars in the world. You'll find weary travellers from all over the Himalayan region as well as from every corner of the globe sipping tea here – yet the place has a monastic feel: hushed, peaceful and meditative. At the point where a spaghetti of roughshod roads meet, the Baralacha La Pass curls its way through a plateau surrounded by mountains and three mesmerising valleys. The popular Suraj Tal trek starts from here. Sarchu – known locally as 'Sir Bhum Chum', the nickname given to Sir Edmund Hillary during the famous climb of Everest in 1953 – feels as if it is skirting the Tibetan border. Sherpas, climbers, overnights and expedition teams all set up camp here and it's easy to pitch a tent as a road-tripper. It is very cold, but if your nether-regions are chilly, a stall selling woven 'Bhum Warmers' has the answer. At an altitude of 4,359 metres (14,300 feet), the panorama is picture-perfect: majestic mountains under milky skies.

Over twenty tight hairpin bends lead to Gata Loops, nestled in the hidden reaches of the Western Himalayas. Reaching this place is a thrill along some skinny stretches bordered by a sheer drop – a challenging terrain that gets the adrenaline pumping. Undulating sweeping views across the entire Ladakh Plateau are the main reason to visit the Lachulung La mountain pass, 5,059 metres (16,597 feet) above sea level and 55 kilometres (34 miles) from Sarchu. Pang is home to the world's highest army transit camp, so expect the bustle of armed forces vehicles and men on the march in this region.

As the highest motorable mountain on the planet, the Tanglang La Pass is a total thrill: the road spirals upwards and it feels like you'll soon reach the clouds. The sweet mountain village of Upshi is set along the Indus River, 45 kilometres (28 miles) south-east of Leh. Almost dedicated to goat farming, it forms part of an ancient trading route linked to Tibet. Karu is hemmed by lofty mountain peaks and steep green hills cut by sparkling streams and bird-filled valleys – park up here to give your limbs a stretch and breathe in a lung-full of crisp, pure air.

Anyone with a passion for adventurous driving will feel utterly exhilarated after journeying the Leh–Manali Highway through one of India's toughest terrains. To me, it felt a real privilege to cross the mighty, spiritual Himalayan Mountains on this most thrilling and highly prized route. I learned new things about myself on this trip when I lost sight of all other vehicles. Time and distance made me feel as if I was the only person on Earth. While part of a motley cavalcade, I drew comfort from the oddball assortment of motorised vehicles around me, but wished them gone. Out of sight, I missed the waves, tooting horns and inane pointing we shared. Mechanical assistance, food and travel tips were traded between us. On one risky section, we whispered a prayer for one another before ploughing through deep water, thick slush and ground that crumbled to dust. Moving branches and debris from the road became physically exhausting. But in the thin air, I knew not to rush. It was imperative to do this trip slowly in order to acclimatise, otherwise headaches, sickness, breathlessness and disorientation can become full-blown Acute Mountain Sickness. Yet, for me, the Leh–Manali Highway is one of those impossibly long, unforgettable road journeys that nag away at you until you do it at least once in a lifetime. Mammoth valleys of rugged rocks peppered with sprouting greenery and ice-topped mountains touching the skies. Wispy clouds, like puffs of breath, form a mysterious swirling script in whey-milk shadows. Dreams are made of this enchanting route – nightmares too.

To avoid the pitfalls of the Highway, pack a decent kit box containing a screwdriver set, small hammer, puncture repair kit, funnel, tow rope, jump-start cables, jack, emergency flares, motor oil and wiper fluid. Get the vehicle serviced and have any niggling problems fixed. Choose a vehicle that can cope with the trip (a 4×4 is best). Carry enough food for several days (chocolate, glucose or other high energy food is good) as well as sunglasses, sunscreen, a torch, drinking water and a spare set of warm clothing.

Watch out for sudden loose gravel on a road surface that ripples like a roller coaster. Thaw skids are frequent. Some roads are frayed like an old bed sheet. Others have turned to slurry. Shifting gravel traps the underbelly of low-slung vehicles. Water crossings (*nallas*) become small rivers after rains. The heaviest downpours can trigger landslides. There's a bitter chill in this cold semiarid desert, but warm sunshine can also pump out intense heat. Make sure you know where petrol is sold (Leh, Karu, Tandi and Manali) and where the hotels and camping are based (Keylong, Sarchu, Manali and Leh). Foreign visitors need permits and everyone has to carry photo ID. And with only one single cash-machine along the entire 480-kilometre (298-mile) route (in Keylong), make sure you take enough cash.

Contacts:
India Tourist Board
www.incredibleindia.org

THE SILK ROAD, UZBEKISTAN

The Silk Road – as much a metaphor for a cultural exchange of ideas, arts and other commodities as a collective network of trading routes – spanned more than 7,400 kilometres (4,600 miles) from eastern China west to the Mediterranean Sea and beyond. Contrary to the name, the route was not one road. Nor was it established solely to enable silk merchants to ply their trade. In fact, a considerable variety of goods were traded across the network of routes, from gold and ivory to exotic animals, plants, precious stones and glass. Religion was another significant commodity. From India,

Photo: Indrajit Das

the Buddhist faith gave birth to a number of different sects across the Central Asian region. Christianity also made an early appearance on the scene. The Silk Road reached the height of its importance during the Tang dynasty from the 7th century, when its role in art and civilisation was immense. Today, the region separating China from Europe and Western Asia may not be as inhospitable as it was in 500–330 BC, but it remains a difficult part of the planet to navigate. Conflict plays its part, as do climate and geography. With very little vegetation, and almost no rainfall, many parts of the route suffer sandstorms, strong winds and extremely harsh climates from summer highs (in the 30s and 40s) and winter lows ($-20°C$). The Silk Road also contains some of the highest mountains in the world.

To meet the challenge, many road-trippers choose to travel a manageable section of what was the Silk Road. My choice was Uzbekistan's colour-packed Golden Road as it passes through a trio of glorious sites of great ancient importance: Bukhara, Samarkand and Tashkent. Once barely on the tourist map, Uzbekistan has captured the imagination of the more adventurous traveller. With its mix of Taj Mahal-esque architecture and the vivid hues of St Petersburg, the tile-work, spires and orb-topped towers are magnificently exotic.

Uzbekistan remains rich in historical artefacts from its favourable position at the centre of the Silk Road routes: it was once one of the most affluent trading kingdoms. The first Chinese who crossed from north to south envied the magnificent Fergana racehorses of Uzbekistan. Once trading began, these big, strong and fast beasts became a valuable part of China's military ambitions. One of the busiest trade routes began in Xi'an, the capital of ancient China, and stretched to its north-west borders along the Gobi Desert and into eastern Turkestan. After crossing the Tien Shan and the Fergana Valley, the route continued west to the Caspian Sea coast. The Silk Road also stretched to Bactria (northern Afghanistan) and India. Another branch went around the Taklamakan Desert from the south and continued on to Persia and Syria to reach the Mediterranean Sea.

Uzbekistan held an enviable strategic location along the Silk Road and was considered an advantageous mercantile hub. This made it prone to attack and the territory of modern Uzbekistan was conquered a number of times by various aggressors. Despite this, the ancient walls of Samarkand, Bukhara and Khiva remain well-preserved, with many grand architectural monuments still beautifully intact. Outside of the city walls, Uzbekistan was also home to nomadic tribes of eagle-hunters who lived in tents and crossed steppes and deserts in pursuit of Mother Nature's legend-steeped bird of prey. Today this strange fusion of East and West, of religion and superstition, underlies Uzbekistan's culture – as if people are pushing forward, but always while looking back.

Nothing prepares you for the beauty of Bukhara, Samarkand and Tashkent. Bukhara, at more than 2,000 years old, is Central Asia's most complete example of a medieval city and is renowned for its 10th-century scholars and artists. Unchanged for centuries, the city is recognised by UNESCO for Outstanding Universal Value. I was wowed by the handsome Kalon Minaret, a 47-metre (154-foot) tower built in 1127 that so impressed Genghis Khan he was moved to spare its destruction – he clearly had some good taste. Other monuments I sought out included the famous tomb of Ismail Samani, a masterpiece of 10th-century Muslim architecture with its striking terracotta brickwork laid over thick stone walls. The ancient Persian city served as a major centre of Islamic culture for many centuries and, despite the destructive invasions of the region by the Mongols (1220) and Timur (1370), this beautiful old town survives unscathed. It is hard not be impressed by Bukhara: it is an architectural triumph and now all new construction has to conform to the traditional style.

Samarkand, renowned throughout Central Asia as a city of myth and fable, is synonymous with the exoticism of the Silk Road. Known as the city of Tamerlane, on account of the man who invested in its ancient prosperity, Samarkand's hero isn't as famous as Genghis Khan, though he was just as ruthless. From his court in Samarkand, Tamerlane, also known as Timur, ruled an empire that stretched from Iraq to western China. He claimed to have killed more than 17 million people and was said to stack the skulls of those he beheaded in giant pyramids. Though Timur was himself a Mongol, not an Uzbek, you'll find statues honouring his name all over town. His body, and those of his family members is the main tourist attraction, and lies in a crypt under the mausoleum.

Tashkent originated as an oasis city on the Silk Road, and became a main link between East and West and one of the richest cities in Central Asia. Today, Tashkent is the largest metropolis in the region, the nation's capital and home to some excellent museums, operas and fine dining. Bordered by rolling agricultural plains on one side and boundless Eurasian step on the other, the fertile lands that surround Tashkent and the waters of the River Chirchik have drawn people for thousands of years. Though it lacks the beauty of Bukhara and Samarkand, the city of Tashkent is attractive, set in the foothills of high mountains on a hilly plain irrigated by gently flowing waters. The city's mishmash mix, to me, is part of its charm. Jaw-dropping exoticism collides with gritty urban sprawl. Refuse spills on to the streets underneath palatial towers topped by domes that look like gilded pepper-pots. Street vendors sell chill-busting Turkmen hats and mobile phones from the same tables (both have a whiff of sheep), while the most vibrant boulevards are blackened by traffic fumes. Hazardous parking and over-filled skips block every sidewalk. And some of the beautiful stucco work, frescoes, turquoise roofs, wrought iron and royal pavilions could do with a deep-clean. Yet Tashkent has an energy and spirit that is almost palpable.

The scenery is an assault on the senses: big, bold and magnificent are closely followed by ramshackle and decrepit. After spectacular glazed tiles in royal blue, yellow and ochre, you'll pass monumental archways in towns dotted with minarets and kaleidoscopic mosaics. Then it's out past piles of hay bales, falling-down farm buildings and out to dusty fields scattered with camels. Robe-clad men wearily scythe arid crops, where solid gold goblets, carved ivory trinkets and lapis beads were once traded. Uzbekistan feels a million miles away from anywhere: it bowled me over, seized my heart and captured my imagination and still hasn't let me go.

Contacts:
Uzbekistan Tourist Board
www.welcomeuzbekistan.uz

FRANKINCENSE ROUTE, OMAN

According to the friendly Omani road-workers mending the curbs in sweltering midday heat, the Bimmah Sinkhole was created by a falling star, not geological erosion. I prefer this poetic explanation and readily claim this belief as my own. The people you meet on your travels can shape your journey. In Oman, as almost everyone speaks English, it is a little easier to engage in road-trip chit-chat – even when you're covering miles and miles of empty desert. Nothing is ever smooth on a roughshod road, which is presumably why the workers were picking at dust. The brain stays on high alert as its rapid responses are tested. The car also shows signs of stress as road conditions challenge each of its mechanical parts. Physiologically, I also feel the strain on this potholed sandy route. My back aches, my palms are sore and I have cramp in my calves. There isn't time to switch off and relax and take a foot off the gas: every metre is like scaling a mountain.

Bordered by the United Arab Emirates, Saudi Arabia and Yemen, the Arab state of Oman is much more than just a desert with incredible natural beauty. Visit the cities and you'll discover a lively food culture using rousing spices, herbs and marinades and a fondness for bright colours and textures. Stroll around the souks to breathe in an awe-inspiring clash of old-fashioned bartering and the electronics and gadgets associated with the most modern aspects of Arabian culture: a weird and wonderful mix.

Sinkholes are still rare in Oman but have become a more occasional hazard in recent times – depending on who you listen to, it's either a symptom of global warming or alien subterfuge. The even terrain means you may not notice a sinkhole until you topple inside, or rattle to a premature halt. Once the front of the bonnet tips forward, awkwardly, I realise the engine is spluttering with good reason. Part of the jeep has plunged down into a pothole the size of a hotel swimming pool. Before me, the road opens up into a sinkhole, attempting to swallow the car in a single gulp. My hands are still gripping the wheel as I stare ahead open mouthed.

It is as if the road is alive, opening its mouth in a yawning growl and gulping. Sinkholes are nothing new in tropical rainy climates like South and Central America: thousands of them develop each year. But in the Middle Eastern desert they are less likely. Irrigation – and lots of it – is more likely to be the cause: thousands of gallons of water each day are pumped on to the desert of the wealthier Arab states in order to transform them into golf course fairways and gardens. Sometimes a slumping tree or sagging fence post can provide an early warning that a sinkhole is forming. Inexplicable pools of water are a red light too. Any bedrock that can naturally dissolve in water is at risk. The ground literally sucks stuff in.

The road in front of me is crumbling away. On closer inspection there's a paper-thin overhang, which has partially peeled back to reveal a honeycomb crater. The earth below looks deflated like a badly cooked soufflé. I slam the jeep into reverse and attempt to exit with caution: staying put is perilous: I could topple into the hole at any second. I gain courage from somewhere as the jeep teeters in a lurching sway. Then, with a rattle and roar, the back tyre gains traction. I breathe again when all four wheels are back on solid ground. Spontaneously, I punch the air before skirting around the hole and continuing on my way.

In a strange coincidence, within about 40 minutes I realise that I am approaching Hawiyat Najm: a crater known to foreigners as the Sinkhole, the Bimmah Sinkhole or the Dabab Sinkhole, but whose name translates to 'The Falling Star'. This hole in the Earth's crust contains fresh water and is much, much larger than 'mine': it is 40 metres (131 feet) wide and plunges 20 metres (65 feet) into cavernous depths. It seems too good a coincidence not to visit, so I swing off the gritty highway. The turning is about 120 kilometres (75

Photo: Hendrik Dacquin

miles) from Muscat, between the capital and the resort town of Sur, but it feels like the end of the Earth.

It has been just three hours since I set off on the 'Frankincense Route' from Muscat, after visiting one of the most iconic mosques in the Middle East: the Sultan Qaboos Grand Mosque. With enough room for 20,000 worshippers, this dome-topped masterpiece is utterly spectacular in every way, from the plush, rich hues of the world's second-largest hand-woven carpet to the dazzling cut-glass chandelier. Now, set between the pinprick villages of Dabab and Bimmah, I am a long way from city planning, traffic signs and road markings. I reach a T-junction and instinctively turn left to follow an unmade road for about five minutes. This is the rural backwaters of Oman at their most isolated, so I am without company except for a few lanky-legged goats nibbling the scrub.

It is just me and the sinkhole.

Wow, it's magical, with its azure waters and unique shimmering green glow. Intrepid types can inch around the rocky ledges that surround the pool and dive straight into the water-filled hollow. Otherwise it's a steep walk down to water level from the top of the crater, though some enterprising soul has added 80 concrete steps to make it less of a slog. The view is striking from the top – the entire sinkhole looks as if it has been plopped down in the desert by mistake. The colours, the texture and the geology look totally out of place. Down at the waterside though, you can stare down into the depths at a squillion tiny fish from the shade of a palm tree. Most passers-by climb into the water-filled crater for a cooling dip: the fish nibble gently at the dry skin on your feet and elbows, raising a giggle if you're ticklish.

As I continue on the highway towards Sur, where I plan to overnight before continuing on to the frankincense town of

Salalah, I reflect on my Omani road-trip thus far. Nothing has quite gone to plan, yet it has been a truly wonderful day. For me, this is the beauty of journeying: the pleasure of the unpredictable. The unexpected. In Oman there are a couple of other surprises for road users: motoring laws that I'm pretty certain can't be found anywhere else. First, it is illegal to drive with a dirty car – nip around with an unwashed auto and you can get pulled over and ticketed. Any level of road rage, even swearing at someone under your breath, is against the law too. A cross word, a gesture or any level of aggression is serious business here. Tomorrow I have an epic eleven-hour drive via Route 31, but in the spirit of Oman, I intend to be a calm and courteous driver all the way.

Contacts:
Oman Tourist Board
www.omantourism.gov.om

THE AMERICAS

ICEFIELDS PARKWAY, CANADA

Also known as Route 93 North, the Icefields Parkway squiggles its way through two of Canada's most spectacular national parks, from the snow-capped alpine town of Jasper– home of SkyTram, Canada's highest and longest aerial tramway – to one of North America's largest ski resorts, Lake Louise. Not only does this beautiful mountain trail cross

Photo: Martin Meyer

through the heart of the Canadian Rocky Mountain Parks to offer mesmerising views of sparkling lakes, limestone cliffs, ancient glaciers and curvaceous valleys, the route is also peppered with mountain goats, elk and bighorn sheep who call the UNESCO World Heritage Site their home. Road-trippers will be struck by the glorious natural colours and pure mountain air of the Icefields Parkway: the blue-pewter of the rocky fjords, the deep blue of the glacial lakes and the glossy green of tufts of foliage. Journeying Icefields Parkway is more than simply travelling a mountain road: it's a route that moulds character, shapes personality and alters the lives of even the most seasoned travellers. As one of the most beautiful journeys on the planet, the Icefields Parkway is ranked as one of the top drives in the world by *Condé Nast Traveller*: a 232-kilometre (144-mile) stretch of double-lane highway that snakes along the Continental Divide through soaring rocky, vast plunging valleys, ice-fields and towering mountain peaks.

Drivers who struggle with concentration at the wheel will be challenged by the constant visual distractions on the Icefields Parkway route. First sparkling turquoise lakes, then tumbling waterfalls, dramatic ancient glaciers and, of course, the glistening splendour of the marble-white Columbia Icefields. All of it is home to bighorn sheep, deer, black bears, coyotes, wolves and grizzly bears and it's not uncommon to spot the silhouette of a mother deer nuzzling her young on a distant horizon. Study the roadside for the tell-tale sign of bear prints.

Fans of TripAdvisor may wish to take note of the feedback posted by those who have journeyed the ice-fields (it ranks as the sixth most popular activity for the region) as one first-hand report after another, with the benefit of hindsight, rues that they foolishly rushed the trip. Without a doubt, the Icefields Parkway deserves a much slower pace than a pedal-to-the-metal road-trip. While it is possible to travel the route in around three hours, it should be a punishable offence to do so. Nobody should clock-watch through this spine-tingling scenery. Nobody. For there is too much to see. Way too much to see. What's more, every mile or so the trailhead signs urge drivers to pull over and give their legs a stretch – a great excuse to delve deeper and explore the spectacular wilderness of the Canadian Rockies.

This stretch of road has more than 100 ancient glacial forests of thick pine and larch trees. Beautifully pure, you feel almost compelled to suck as much of the air into your lungs as possible for curative or therapeutic rewards. The highlight, if it is possible to pinpoint one utterly unmissable single sight, has to be Peyto Lake (the locals pronounce it 'pea-toe'), a much-photographed fjord fed by glacial water and an intense kingfisher blue. The vibrancy is mind-blowing and proof that the glossy photographs published in coffee-table books, travel brochures and postcards all over the world have not been enhanced by software trickery. It may well be the most beautiful lake on Earth on account of its blue colour, caused by the glacial sediment. Each day, each hour even, the colour alters. The tourist board insists that the best views of the lake are from the Bow Summit – a well-signed lookout point just off the Parkway itself (around 40 kilometres/25 miles from Lake Louise). A car park marks the start of a steep paved trail up to the lookout, which takes about fifteen minutes at a steady slog. But there is a much better viewpoint a little further along from here up a makeshift trail – look carefully and you'll see it tucked within the trees. For two minutes extra walking, you'll be away from any other tourists with astounding views from a plateau with no platform (and therefore nothing to stop you from toppling over the edge). It is so beautiful that it is almost spiritual: a heavenly and tranquil spot in which the reflecting properties of the water are hypnotic. Named after Bill Peyto, an English explorer who first discovered it in 1894, the Lake sits within Banff National Park, in an area that is home to marmots, picas and ptarmigans.

With nothing to divert the eyes for miles and miles, other than the views, your mind can wander from topics like the Ice Age to the power of the sun's reflections without interruption. An hour can easily pass as you stare into the lake's waters – so clear that you can practically see to the bottom of its 90-metre (295-foot) depth. Salmon, brook trout and channel catfish thrive here without the worry of pollution. Around the lake look for lodgepole pine, and a pretty five-petal alpine variant of one of the 50 or so species of forget-me-nots. Other memorable flora on or around the Parkway include moss campion and small white-and-yellow dryas. With a pair of decent binoculars you may even spot the park's rare golden eagles soaring across the ice-milled passes and ledges of the surrounding range.

Few other spots cause such wide-eye wonder as Lake Peyto, but there are plenty that come close. The Athabasca Falls, about 30 kilometres (19 miles) from Jasper, are a fine example of powerful pounding waterfalls, while in the Sunwapta Valley, around 98 kilometres (61 miles) from Jasper, the glass-floored Glacier Sky Walk, which opened in 2014, boasts bird's eye views from 280 metres (919 feet) – but be warned, it feels like walking on thin air. Parker Ridge, 110 kilometres (68 miles) from Jasper, offers a lung-busting two-hour hike to the Saskatchewan Glacier. About 150 kilometres (93 miles) from Jasper, at the confluence of the mighty North Saskatchewan River, the Howse River and the Mistaya River, a spot known locally as 'The Crossing' denotes the starting point of the Columbia Icefield.

Contacts:
Canada Tourist Board
www.canada.travel

HISTORIC ROUTE 66, USA

Legions of road-trippers dream of getting their kicks on Route 66, usually bathed in glorious sunshine in an open-topped Corvette. Millions, like me, have been captivated by this legendary long-distance route. Slicing through the heart of the USA on a diagonal course between Chicago and Los Angeles, Route 66 is blessed with archetypal American kitsch. From dusty saloon bars and rusty truck stops to neon-lit signs and roadside diners, Route 66 navigates a historic road traversed by adventurers from every walk of life. From old travellers and dreamers to fugitives and schemers, Route 66 offers everything from lowlife to the high life (as well as plenty of wildlife), which is why it has been dubbed the Mother Road.

While the actual on-the-map Route 66 no longer officially exists, a considerable proportion of the journey through all eight states can still be retraced. Parts of it are still signed Route 66 to help road-trippers stay on-track and a considerable support network of businesses and attractions has sprung up around the legend over the years. Though some roadside treasures have disappeared, a number of preservation organisations dedicate themselves to conserving many of the original landmarks. After all, there's a queue of vehicles from every corner of the globe keen to drive the most famous road-trip on Earth – drivers of the world unite on the subject of Route 66.

Photo: CT.Liotta

Route 66 was born out of a growing nation keen to follow aspirations and dreams and discover unexplored lands. America had started to expand westward and the rolling countryside beyond the Mississippi River had captured the imagination of Americans keen to seek fresh fortune. Initially hindered by the lack of easily navigable paths, they soon blazed trails themselves where eventually wagons then trains would roll. A transportation corridor began to emerge that expanded once the automobile arrived – and changed America forever. Once cars became affordable to the ordinary person, Americans really began to travel. Long-distance journeys that would have taken days by horse or wagon became doable in a day. Road surfaces were mainly dirt tracks across vast sections of America. Improvements were steady, with around 2 per cent paved by the early 20th century and a growing voice for a standardised National Highway System. By 1921, changes to the Federal Aid Road Act necessitated road upgrade and introduced Oklahoma businessmen Cyrus Avery – now known to many as the father of Route 66 – to the scene. Avery became one of the strongest supporters of the Chicago to Los Angeles route, which he wanted to follow the Old Santa Fé Trail and would pass his home town. He lobbied for a route that would wind 2,400 miles (3,862 kilometres) through the most romantic and celebrated portions of the American West to connect the small Midwestern towns of Illinois, Missouri and Kansas with the big cities of Los Angeles and Chicago. Cutting through a diverse cross-section of American scenery, it runs from the cornfields of Illinois all the way to the golden sands and sunshine of Los Angeles. And when you grasp that it contains such diverse landscapes within its scope as the Grand Canyon, the South-West desert, the small-town Midwest heartlands and the high-rise towers of Chicago, well, it almost makes you gasp for breath.

A new era of road-building followed that inspired a nation, created mass excitement, significant employment and carried a nation on the move through hard times, war and recovery. Route 66 – a uniquely American road – secured a special place in the hearts of the American people. It symbolised the country's new and passionate love affair with the automobile: a deep and lasting affection that endures to this day.

Today Route 66 is synonymous with spirited adventure and freedom on the open road. It also offers those who drive it a voyage through the timeline of contemporary America. By the late 1950s, development saw it bypassed section by section as the network of high-speed Interstate highways were built. In 1984, Route 66 was officially decommissioned and has since been designated Historic Route 66. Though it is no longer an official main route across the country, Route 66 has retained its allure. It was the first route in the USA that used roadside billboards for promotion and road-trippers today are still entertained by a bamboozling array of kooky advertising hoardings. Nostalgia-seekers journey Route 66 landmarks keen to relive old memories, while first-time road-trippers ride this idiosyncratic route to experience the old through the new. With one foot in the past, and another in the future, Route 66 offers an unforgettable journey into America, both then and now. Though only 85 per cent of the road has survived, its spirit lives on – as I know first hand. In a gleaming eight-berth Winnebago, with a Beach Boys CD for company, I drove this iconic road tailed by a line of hand-polished Mustangs, Fords and Chevys. As I cruised through each classic mile of authentic Americana, crossing a trio of time zones, it felt like I was on a shortcut to freedom. With a few sticks of gum, some twenty dollar bills and a lifetime of dreams in my pocket.

Contacts:
Route 66, USA
www.visittheusa.com

TRANS-ANDEAN HIGHWAY, SOUTH AMERICA

Wispy cloud, milky skies and scrub-topped mountains characterise most of the Andes Mountain region and this helter-skelter highway spirals from Santiago in Chile to the wine region of Mendoza in Argentina. Tight, winding descents and gear-crunching climbs demand nerves of steel as vehicles teeter on the edge of skinny roads over deep valleys of ragged rocks. Anyone who suffers from car sickness may want to give this trip a miss because some of the twists and turns are stomach-turning – and the arresting views are little help once the sick bag comes out. Still, the wonder, awe and challenges of the journey have a suitably spectacular ending – through a 3-kilometre (2-mile) tunnel that catapults your vehicle into the handsome vine-terraces of rural Argentina. The rest of the road-trip is all downhill, which is when the terrifying freewheeling and braking start!

Embarking on any part of this trip, in whole or in part, requires expedition planning – for it is not a simple day's jaunt in the car. It is cold, very cold, which can come as a shock because the lower foothills of the Andes are hot, muggy and airless. But once you start scaling the scenic slopes towards the most remote little cloud-topped Andean villages, the temperature plummets. Each stage of the elevation takes you through a contrasting hotchpotch of vegetation zones on the rutted spines, velvety folds, scrubby peaks and rounded curves of one of the longest mountain ranges on Earth. Stretching over 7,080 kilometres (4,400 miles) along the west coast of South America, the Andes pass through seven nations: Argentina, Bolivia, Chile, Colombia, Ecuador, Peru and Venezuela (if you are listing them A-to-Z). Forming a massive barrier between the eastern Pacific Ocean and the rest of the South American continent, this ragged ridge is a major force in controlling the wildly varying climatic disparities of the entire region. From the hot, steamy lowlands and humid rain-forests close to the equator to the frozen plains nearer to the Antarctic and the scarcely populated grassy slopes and rocky streams that rumble down glacially carved valleys.

It is common to map the soaring peaks of the Andes into three natural regions: the southern, central and north. In the northern part of the Andes (Venezuela, Colombia and Ecuador) the climate is typically rainy and warm. The Central Andes are extremely arid and include the Atacama Desert in northern Chile as well as Peru and Bolivia; the eastern portion of the Central Andes is much wetter. The Southern Andes (Chile and Argentina) are rainy and cool. Many of the peaks in the Andes are snow-topped and contain glaciers, though these have lost mass over the last three decades.

My chosen route – the Trans-Andean Highway – will take me from Mendoza, Argentina across mountain roads to Valparaiso, Chile: a journey that benefits from an early start to take full advantage of a first day's drive in daylight. In good weather, when the route isn't blocked by wildlife, accident or road repairs, crossing the pass should take about eight hours. Even the most experienced road-tripper shouldn't try night-driving in the Andes, so an important part of the drive is continuous momentum along a route that ranks pretty highly on the list of the '10 Most Dangerous Drives in the World'.

Photo: Mario Gonzalez

It takes a good four hours until you reach the scary part of the Trans Andean Highway at the top of the pass. Before that you criss-cross swollen rivers on a steady climb towards the snow on the mountains. At one point, you can sense the intimidating presence of the tallest mountain in the Americas, the mighty Aconcagua at 6,961 metres (22,838 feet). It's while driving this particularly bleak, desolate stretch that you realise there will be no long hot day in the car. The cold is biting and you start to shiver as the mountains get pointier and more jagged.

At the highest point, a gloomy tunnel carries you from Argentina into Chile. A sign saying 'Welcome to Chile' confirms you've made it to the other side. From here it's all downhill and where the scary roads start – steep and set at a crazy angle so your vehicle is in a permanent tilt. After clearing customs at border control (which takes about an hour), the road gets even steeper and starts to spiral in a terrifying succession of tight circles: all in all there are around twenty extremely sharp hairpin bends. No barriers. No lane markings. Just lots of big trucks rumbling up behind you and blasting their horns to encourage you to increase your speed. Then just as you think the bends are going to stop, road signs announce the road is narrowing even further due to construction. Some bits are half-paved. And on the skinniest bits there is no alternative but to drive on the wrong side of the road facing oncoming traffic. It requires something special not to panic when there's a sheer drop alongside you and a head-on collision coming your way. I had a sudden urge to give my nails a chew, but was too terrified to peel either palm from the wheel.

Through the fogged-up car window, the plants that thrive in this unique place look extraordinary: hardy, resilient and tough in order to survive this harsh environment. Many are very small, to conserve energy. Others are stiff and robust, to withstand brutal winds and frosts. One of the biggest threats to the landscape of the Andean region is land clearance, both legal and illegal, for pastureland, as well as overgrazing and wide-scale burning. In the lower elevations, the coffee, rice, sugar cane and soy that grow rely on water from the Andes' higher slopes. Cloud-forest in most remote areas is often used to grow coca for cocaine, marijuana and opium poppy for heroin. Expensive attempts to control the drug crops by spraying chemicals from light aircraft have had minimal success. Drug supply has been unaffected, but the chemical deluge has killed livestock, made children sick and decimated the natural ecosystems of the Andes. Ecuador, Peru and Bolivia are also planning road-building programmes that will destroy massive amounts of Andean forest.

Although the heater is on, the cold is bone-chilling even though the zip of my coat is closed tight up to my chin. I huddle into my thick, woolly scarf as though I am braving winter in the Scottish Highlands. All around it is green, windswept and wild: a very good reason why some of the specialist outdoor clothing brands test their gear out here. My toes are numb as I survey the pea-green misty canvas of the Andes. As soon as the road straightens and my shoulders relax a little, I blow on my hands and rub them together and drive through damp marshmallow clouds.

South America's most important cities, namely Bogotá, Quito, Sucre, Arequipa, Medellín and La Paz, are all located in the Andes. At 6,920 kilometres (4,300 miles) in length, the mountains vary from around 193 kilometres (120 miles) wide to almost 724 kilometres (450 miles) at their widest points. In height, they average around 4,000 metres (13,123 feet). The Andes contain enormous mineral wealth and yield vast quantities of copper, silver and gold. The mountains are home to 30,000 plant species, 600 known mammal species, more than 1,700 species of bird, over 600 types of reptiles and 400 species of fish. The highest mountain range outside Asia, the Andes are twice the length of the Himalayas. Apart from a border control guard and some truck drivers, in five hours I haven't seen another human soul.

Nor have I spotted the giant wingspan or oversized shadow of the Andean condor: a large and majestic specimen that the whole of South America holds dear. As national symbols of Colombia, Ecuador, Peru, Bolivia, Chile and Argentina, largely because of the mystical importance attached to them by indigenous ethnic groups, condors have a commanding presence: nesting at altitudes of 3,658 metres (12,000 feet) or more they can live for up to 70 years. This single bird species embodies the Andes and has been an important symbol since pre-colonial times, when indigenous tribes-folk considered them messengers of the gods and harbingers of good fortune.

Soaring to 4,572 metres (15,000 feet), and flying over 241 kilometres (150 miles) a day, a condor can pinpoint a potential meal from on high. They are well-adapted for feeding on carrion, with a head with very few feathers it can easily get into rotting carcasses with minimal mess. Sharp bill and talons help it to tear muscles and viscera through the skin of the largest carcasses. When they have eaten enough, Andean condors clean their bald heads by scraping them along the ground to remove any food scraps. They aren't beautiful, with mottled deep-pink bare skin and fleshy caruncle, but they are strong, silent and – weighing up to a whopping 15 kilograms (33 pounds) – the largest raptors on Earth. At one time the Andean condor could be found along the entire western coast of South America from Venezuela to the southern tip of Patagonia. Today it is mainly seen in the higher peaks of the Andes, from western Venezuela to Tierra del Fuego. I tear my eyes from the sky and focus on the road ahead: the tight bends are behind me and I am nearing my final destination. It's time to stop looking for Andean condors because if I get the braking wrong, or choose a wrong gear, the car will flip into a deep-cut canyon...

Contacts:
Andean Cultural website
www.andes.org.uk

THE ALASKA HIGHWAY, CANADA TO ALASKA

Constructed during the Second World War, in just eight frenzied months in 1942, the 'Alcan' (as the route is commonly known) was built to protect the north-west flank of North America from Japanese invasion. The road had to be built, no matter what. So more than 17,000 men were put to work on round-the-clock construction duty, using over 7,000 trucks and bulldozers and erecting 133 bridges along the way. In temperatures ranging from 90°F to –70°F, workers had to contend with humid forests, swamps, rivers, ice, mosquitoes, flies and the biting cold. The naturally warm bubbling waters of the Liard River Hot Springs Provincial Park (Mile 496) made Mile 496 the most popular posting with construction crews. Today this challenging mountain drive slices through snow-capped mountains along a potentially perilous route. Twisting and turning for over 2,232 kilometres (1,387 miles), the road is characterised by snow drifts, ice sheets and far-reaching summits. Goats roam free in the middle of the road under snow-capped rocky brown mountains, while sheep lick the salt at the edge of purple-blue lakes. Beautiful birds linger on snow-heavy boughs in dark-green spruce forests. Mysterious trails lead to sun-lit glaciers and curious gape-mouthed caves.

The Mile 0 marker denotes the start of the Alaska Highway in Dawson Creek, British Columbia. The official end of the Alaska Highway is Delta Junction, historic milepost 1422. It's one heck of a slog that's roughly the equivalent of a trip from London to Moscow. Despite the name, two-thirds of the road is actually in Canada.

Full-throttle drivers could complete the route in a day-and-a-half if they drive it non-stop. However, most visitors pack their thick-soled boots to take advantage of some of the hikes along the way. Packing up the car for a trip up the Alaska Highway requires proper planning for this is no simple drive to the park. This pioneer road traverses a vast wilderness in a remote expanse of North America. Consider the weather conditions, the wildlife, the vehicle and your warmth and safety, and keep in mind that road repairs are almost year-round on this mammoth stretch. Asphalt surfacing on the Alaska Highway ranges from dreadful to excellent: with the average 'fair'. So you'll need to be prepared for potholes and loose gravel, and to pack a puncture repair kit.

The first 483 kilometres (300 miles) of highway, between Dawson Creek and Fort Nelson, are simple and straight. They run through grassy fields and farmland along the riverside Kiskatinaw Provincial Park, near a historic wooden curved trestle bridge. The river is used as the local swimming baths, with stretches also fished, and the park is beautifully maintained by a spirited bunch of local volunteers. North of Fort Nelson, the Alaska Highway crosses the Rocky Mountains and tapers to a skinny road for around 241 kilometres (150 miles) to cross Summit Pass (Historic Milepost 392 and the highest summit on the Alaska Highway at 1,295 metres/4,250 feet) and continues on a winding route to the MacDonald River valley. The Alaska Highway drops steeply at this limestone gorge: a dramatic setting that is home to a scruffy-haired bunch of stone sheep, a subspecies of thinhorn sheep. Further north, a pure white subspecies known as Dall sheep predominates. There are plenty of wildlife hazards here, with caribou bounding out of roadside forests. At the other side of the valley, the Alaska Highway shoots out on a 708-kilometre (440-mile) stretch to Whitehorse via Watson Lake. Squeezed between the rolling hills of south-east Yukon, Watson Lake is one of the most reliable spots to witness the dancing strobes of colour of the spectacular Aurora Borealis (Northern Lights). It is home to the Northern Lights Space and Science Centre and is a convenient gateway to the breathtaking scenery of Yukon. Look out for the Signpost Forest here: a bizarre collection of more than 60,000 signs – road signs, name signs, markers and mottoes – from around the world. The first sign was put up in 1942 by a homesick G.I., and now the stop here is a tradition. Whitehorse, the capital of Yukon Territory, is close to the basalt cliffs of Miles Canyon, site of a former gold-rush town. From the canyon, the Yukon River Loop Trail winds north, past the Whitehorse Fishway fish ladder towards the S.S. *Klondike*, a restored sternwheeler that once plied the Yukon River. A hundred miles from here, Haines Junction is a 322-kilometre (200-mile) straight road to the Alaska border – a fast stretch that races to the frontier at full-pelt.

The Alaska Highway is driven year-round, although most tourist traffic hits the road between May and September. Expect cold nights (freezing and below) by early September

in parts of the Yukon and interior Alaska. It is common for businesses to be seasonal. If you're travelling in winter, carry a block heater and emergency road gear as well as warm blankets. Studded tyres will help avoid traction challenge in unploughed snow. Always travel with a full tank of fuel and keep a spare jerrycan in the boot because whiteouts and below zero temperatures are common in the winter months. It's always a good idea to book accommodation ahead. Small to mid-sized communities along the Alaska Highway may only have a few rooms. RV parks and campgrounds along the Alaska Highway are plentiful – 23 at last count.

All sorts of vehicles journey the Alaska Highway in summer, from bicycles, motorcycles, vintage and compact cars to pop-up trailers, motorhomes and trucks. To cross the border, you'll need to present travel documents (visa and passport) and an international driving licence. As you'll be travelling through two different countries, you'll need currencies for both. You'll find banks in Dawson Creek, Fort St John, Fort Nelson, Watson Lake, Whitehorse, Tok, Delta Junction and Fairbanks. Fuel, food and lodging are found in towns and cities along the Alaska Highway (though there can be as much as 241 kilometres/150 miles in between). Not many are open for 24 hours. Long stretches of the Alaska Highway are without a cell phone service. Satellite phone networks can be rented in Whitehorse. Apart from in and around the larger towns, the route is largely unlit. On the darkest coal-black stretches look out for the glow of wolves' eyes in the night – younger pups shine a beautiful blue and fully grown adults glow pale yellow, amber and bright orange.

Contacts:
Alaskan Tourism
www.travelalaska.com

COASTAL HIGHWAY 15, MEXICO

Cactus-scattered sandy scrub and oven-hot breezes characterise the early stretches of Mexico's Coastal Highway 15, an exotic terrain that becomes more beautifully feral once you've crossed the border from Arizona. Unlike some nightmare frontiers, Nogales is fuss-free: simply present your papers and passport at the crossing, start up your motor and cruise into Mexico. A large metal road sign bids you welcome to the state of Sonora. Another points the way to Mexico City – a 3,478-kilometre (2,161-mile) drive.

The first thing to mention is that Mexican drivers are more aggressive behind the wheel than Americans – horns and wild gesticulations are used more than brakes and indicators. Speed is an integral part of Mexico's driving culture and before any Mexican road-trip it pays to brush up on the rules of the road, from the strict laws of the freeway to the unspoken lane-changing customs. Roads vary in condition, from multi-million-dollar highways (usually toll roads called *cuotas*) and routes littered with unmarked *topes* (speed bumps) to bone-jarring moon-cratered backroads. Turn signals are rarely used. Many country roads are full of people riding wobbly cycles and livestock on the roam. Overtaking is arbitrary. Changing lanes a lottery. Attempting a left-hand turn is perilous. Two-lane highways with hard shoulders double as four-lane routes. Potholes are cavernous. Although signs stating 'no exceda los límites de velocidad' are common, speed limits are meaningless. Cars have no respect or duty of care to each other. Conversely, it is truck drivers who are Mexico's courteous kings of the road.

If you have a choice of cars, opt for the least flashy model in Mexico. It is also wise to avoid driving at night – not

just because of car-jacking, but because of the state of the roads. Driving in the daylight is easier and a safer bet. Keep a note of the numbers to call in the event of an accident – 066 (the equivalent of 999 or 111) and 078 (the Green Roadside assistance number for toll roads only). Unleaded fuel (*magna*) is from a green pump at fuel stations. The higher octane super is in the red. It's customary to tip the attendant a few pesos because they will probably also offer to check the oil, fill the tyres with air and wipe a wet cloth over the windscreen.

Nogales, the Mexican border town, has the quaint feel of Old America coupled with Latino vibrancy and offers the unique cultural, linguistic and culinary mix that international frontiers bring. For thousands of years, Nogales has formed part of the migratory path and trade route much later called El Camino Real (The King's Highway). Regiments of armour-clad Conquistadors later forayed north along this valley in quest of precious metals and gems – you can still see missions built by the Spanish colonials. In fact architecture buffs will relish the variety of building styles in and around Nogales, from the predominant Sonoran vernacular to some fine examples of Queen Anne cottage, second empire, Spanish colonial, pueblo revival, Mediterranean and pretty red-roofed bungalows: a reflection of the influences of Native American, Hispanic and Anglo cultures on the history of the city.

As you leave the hammock, ceramic pot and copper sellers and the handcraft stalls of Nogales behind, you'll see signs for Kino Bay, a water-sports spot popular with American weekenders that has first-rate boating conditions. For the next 386 kilometres (240 miles), the route heads coastward with its sights on the Gulf of Mexico.

First stop is Hermosillo, the capital of the state of Sonora, and one of the most attractive cities in northern Mexico. Just

269 kilometres (167 miles) from the United States' border, Hermosillo's picturesque Plaza Zaragoza is much-visited by international tourists, but the number one attraction is the Ecological Center. This enormous showcase brings together a wide variety of flora and fauna from the various ecosystems of Sonora – the highlight is a dazzling collection of beautiful botanical gardens with 300 categories of sweet-smelling and indigenous plants.

Next it is on to the fishing port city of Guaymas, founded by the Spanish in 1769 and set on the Sea of Cortez. It is the home of one of Mexico's most important carnival celebrations and an exciting place for an overnight stop. Of the cities that you pass through during the Highway 15 road-trip, Guaymas is one of the most charming. A settlement renowned for its rural traditions, you'll find textile weavers here with their red, green, gold and bold blue threads crafting magnificent rugs in dazzling Aztec designs. Sombrero-clad farmers navigate horse-pulled carts of crops across bumpy fields. In the hearts, minds and stomachs of Mexicans nationwide, Guaymas is also synonymous with great-tasting seafood, particularly the succulent *camaromes gigantes* (massive shrimp). It seemed only right to stop at a seafood restaurant here for lunch in the elegant Plaza de los Tres Presidentes and eat my fill.

The sprawling metropolis of Ciudad Obregón welcomes over 30 million passers-through each year, on their way to scenic mountains and the coast. Now a popular all-year-round tourist destination in its own right, Ciudad Obregón boasts a deep-rooted history stemming from ethnic Yaqui peoples who fiercely defended their culture from the Spanish colonists in the 1700s. Today, the Yaqui continue to practise traditional medicine using herbs, nuts, seed and sap. Dance rituals and music unique to this indigenous tribe play a very important role in Ciudad Obregón's day-to-day culture in harmony with the regular family-focused theatrical performances held at the city's popular Oscar Russo Theater. Unfortunately, I arrived to hot sunny skies and the truck stop tail-end of a violent sandstorm, so I only saw my surroundings from the window of my hotel.

Whizz past Los Mochis – an urban truck stop on the Ferrocarril Chihuahua al Pacífico that links with ferries to Baja California – unless you need to stop for fuel. Give Culiacán a similarly wide berth, because it is home to the wealthiest drug lords in Mexico, conveniently nestled between the Pacific Ocean and the Sierra Madre mountains just a two-day drive from the US border. You'll see the city is a showcase for luxury homes, prosperous business, modern roads and souvenirs that celebrate the outlaw culture of Los Mochis – medallions of the patron saint of drug smuggling, Jesús Malverde, are the most popular purchase.

The road to Mazatlán entices drivers with alluring images of spectacular beaches on hoardings by the side of the road. Yet nothing prepares you for the real-life beauty of a sweeping 20-kilometre (12-mile) stretch of sandy beaches: a golden ribbon that forms a striking backdrop to Mazatlán's tropical neoclassical historic core. Mazatlán is a lively resort town in the state of Sinaloa and its harbour is renowned for big-game fishing. In its historic centre, 19th-century landmarks include the performance hall Teatro Ángela Peralta and the towering Immaculate Conception basilica. The modern district of Zona Dorada is known for its nightlife and high-rise hotels. Don't miss an opportunity to stroll along the classic sea-front *malecón* (promenade), where old-fashioned bars and restaurants with sunset views evoke the charm of Mexico past.

Next, the city of Tepic, a settlement founded by the nephew of Hernán Cortés in 1524 and the capital of Nayarit state. A genteel place, it has a well-heeled provincial bustle in and around its regal main plaza. Under the arches by the Palacio Municipal (City Hall), the indigenous Huicholes in their brightly coloured clothing sell beaded handicrafts from blankets on the ground. The city's Church of the Cruz de Zacate is a pilgrimage site for Catholics region-wide as home to the legendary cross of grass to which miracles are attributed – expect massive crowds of devotees over Lent and Easter.

For a heady mix of tequila and traditional Mexican mariachi bands, take time to explore the city of Guadalajara, capital of western Mexico's Jalisco state. As a prelim to Mexico's size, scale and intensity, Guadalajara is a toe in the water. It also has the origins for a whole slew of clichés associated with Mexican culture. You'll find rodeos, big moustaches and wide-brimmed sombreros here, which more than compensate for the city's lack of intimacy. It's a huge place with some notable buildings, including the Instituto Cultural de Cabañas, a UNESCO World Heritage site. Upscale restaurants, fashionable boutiques and chichi cafes have earned the city the nickname Mexico's Beverly Hills.

Toluca, which is the capital of the state of Mexico, is located on the fringes of Mexico City, an hour from the city centre. Known as 'La Bella', it is the highest city in Mexico (2,696 metres/8,844 feet above sea level). It has handsome 19th-century colonial architecture, and is home of the oh-so-delicious sausage taco – a handy thing to know if your stomach rumbles as you approach the turning into town. Toluca's international airport is one of Mexico's most important hubs with domestic flights to Cancún, Los Cabos, Monterrey and Puerto Vallarta, and international flights to Los Angeles, Houston and Oakland. From Toluca an excellent toll road runs straight into Mexico City. One of the largest metropolitan areas on the planet with sixteen residential boroughs and with more than 300 neighbourhoods, this is a city on an overwhelming scale. Once the ancient Aztec city of Tenochtitlán, Mexico City was originally built over the ancient Lake Texcoco in the Valley of Mexico. Most of the Aztec structures and canals were destroyed when the Spanish arrived in 1519. Today the finest remaining examples of ancient Aztec city planning can be found at the Teotihuacán archaeological site, 50 kilometres (31 miles) north-east of the city.

Contacts:
Mexico Tourist Board
www.visitmexico.com

BADLANDS NATIONAL PARK, USA

As one of America's lesser known National Parks, the rugged beauty of the Badlands remains much underrated, a result of being eclipsed, I suspect, by the reputations of its bigger, brasher siblings, such as Yellowstone and the Grand Canyon. Yet there are plenty of good times to be had in the Badlands, something that a growing number of visitors from around the world have woken up to. With its striking geologic deposits, the park's 381 square miles (987 square kilometres), where ancient mammals such as the rhino, horse and sabre-toothed cat once roamed, is fossil-rich. Today, a large expanse of mixed-grass prairie is home to bison, bighorn sheep, prairie dogs, mule deer, antelope and black-footed ferrets. Oh, and a thriving population of coyotes.

Badlands National Park is located 75 miles (121 kilometres) east of Rapid City, South Dakota and is reached via the

Interstate 90 (I-90). The Highway 240 Badlands Loop Road is extremely well-signed from whatever direction you drive and is accessed by a two-lane paved road that runs through the northern section of the park. It really couldn't be simpler. That doesn't stop a large number of domestic road-trippers, however, on a jaunt from South Dakota to Montana, from whizzing straight by and missing this awesome drive.

For me, part of the appeal of the Badlands National Park Loop is that it is easy to drive: proof that not every incredible road-trip needs to have an element of jeopardy. It provides a great introduction to America's system of national parks. Relentless beauty, mile after mile. Smooth roads. You can take your eyes off the road here. You can also dip in and out on a mix of side-roads. Cut it short or go around again – it's entirely up to you. I drove it twice, once in each direction.

It doesn't take long to realise that parts of the Badlands are like something out of a *Star Trek* movie and there is a compulsion to stop at every lookout and wooden boardwalk to snap a shot for posterity. Spectacular roads less travelled, full of higgledy-piggledy rocks and canyons of curious shapes, are alive with weird-looking bighorn sheep. The landscape, raw and rugged, harks back to a prehistoric era and makes you wonder how on earth earlier settlers ever survived. Gaping cracks in orange clay-rich soil are backed by vivid brick-red peaks with shrivelled ochre-coloured riverbeds in serpentine squiggles. Layers of red-and-yellow palaeosols (fossilised soils) contain root traces, burrows, animal bones and mineral deposits. The mind-blowing intensity of the deep amber and scarlet is almost overpowering to the naked eye. Binoculars help to scale it in and draw it in for closer scrutiny. And you shouldn't need too much forensic examination of the horn-like tree and rock spikes to spot solitary golden eagles perched above a maze of buttes, canyons, pinnacles and

Photo: Chris Light

spires. Stretches of road are roughshod stones, others prone to snow drifts. Some close in wet weather. You don't need a jeep or 4×4, although it is probably a more comfortable trip in a high clearance vehicle. Signs will indicate if certain trails are only passable in dry conditions or doable in wet or under snow.

So why does a land this spellbinding have such a bad reputation? The Sioux people were the first to call this place 'mako sica' or 'land bad' – and the name just stuck. It suited this exposed terrain of extreme temperatures and drought: the early fur trappers of the 19th century added weight to the reputation by describing it as 'les mauvais terres pour traverser', or 'bad lands to travel through'. Ongoing erosion, at a rate of one inch a year, continues to re-define this changeable landscape. Gullies, ridges, trails and chasms alter. Twisted spires disappear. Each view and each trail will be different the next time you visit. So consign the most gasp-inducing scenery to memory (and photograph) by taking the time to fully explore the Pinnacles Overlook (the highest peak on the Badlands Loop Road at 3,625 feet/1,105 metres), Conata Basin Overlook and the Norbeck Pass area. And if you are a sucker for amazing sunsets, be sure to walk a section of the Castle Trail where the ethereal changing lights and berry-coloured glows of the north side of the Badlands wall is reminiscent of the Northern Lights.

To fully experience most of what the Badlands has to offer, be sure to allow two days to road-trip the park: this allows you freedom to stop at every viewpoint without watching the clock. Set aside time to spend at the Sage Creek Rim Road or the Wilderness Area to watch bison, prairie dogs, bighorn sheep and other creatures). Hiking a rugged backcountry trail is also a wonderful adventure (there are five routes, ranging from a moderate walk of a mile-and-a-half to a full-day's strenuous trek) as is a walk in the company of a fossil expert – the White River area contains a rich bounty of late Eocene and Oligocene fossils. Research in the area has formed the basis of vertebrate palaeontology in North America, with numerous important finds providing evidence of ancient animals from different geologic time periods. Oligocene fossils include those of camels, three-toed horses, oreodonts, antelope-like animals, rhinoceroses, deer-like mammals, rabbits, beavers, creodonts, land turtles, rodents and birds. Marine fossils, from an ancient sea dating from 75 to 67 million years ago during the Cretaceous period, include nautiloids, fish, marine reptiles and turtles, unearthed in Badland's Pierre Shale and Fox Hills formations. Vertebrate fossils preserved within the White River Badlands have been studied extensively since 1846 and are included in museum collections throughout the world. I scoured the rocks of the canyons and ravines for the tell-tale ram's horn shape of an ammonite, with its upward coiling spirals. Visually, the Badlands are at their best early or late in the day, when deep shadows define their forms. And when the light began to dim I forgot all about fossils; soon I was utterly captivated by the sunset.

Contacts:
Badlands National Park
USA National Park Service
www.nps.gov

SAN JUAN SKYWAY, USA

Nothing prepares a driver for the sheer density of the autumn colours in the San Juan Mountains – they are so spectacular it is tricky to fully focus on the road. Time it right, and the seasonal splendour and heraldic hues will be on full display as you road-trip along the San Juan Skyway Scenic Byway: an eight-hour route that takes you on a 236-mile (380-kilometre) loop through a landscape rich in aspens, bubbling hot springs and historic ghost towns. Set off in South-West Colorado from Ouray to Ridgway before hitting Telluride, through Dolores, Cortez and Durango. Then it's back along the Highway 550 for the oh-so-classic Million Dollar Highway section between Silverton and Ouray – so named because of the mesmerising, priceless views. The route climbs to 10,000 feet (3,048 metres) to what feels like the top of the world on the San Juan Skyway – in fact the mountains boast 1,000 peaks above 10,000 feet (including 14 of the 54 peaks in Colorado over 14,000 feet/4,267 metres). At 14,150 feet (4,313 metres), Mount Sneffels is the highest peak of the Sneffels Range, part of the San Juan Mountains distinctive for their lava and ash mineral-laden formations sculpted by glaciers. Though mined extensively, just a small proportion of Mount Sneffels's riches have been extracted – the rest remain buried deep in the mountain.

Once you've hit Ridgway on the clockwise loop, head north on US-550 for Ridgway State Park – part of a region dubbed the 'Switzerland of America'. Here, the distant snow-capped peaks of the San Juan Mountains can be seen from the banks of the grass-fringed Ridgway Reservoir: an idyllic spot to swim, fish, camp and breathe in the pure air of Mother Nature, or pan for gold. Each season brings a different atmosphere, with autumn lending it intensely vibrant splashes of colour. Baronial hues, warmed by the penetrating golden rays of the late summer sun sitting low in the sky, adorn the terrain, with bronze, gold, crimson, burgundy and cardinal red glistening like jewels and gilt.

Toadstools and other bizarre-looking fungi sprout up from hollows and knotted tree roots nourished by the colour-rich leafy carpet. You may also see vivid berry tones and splashes of saffron and orange in among the buttery-gold and auburn glows. Shorter days and cooler nights signal it is time for wildlife to prepare for the winter months in this kaleidoscopic array of autumn foliage.

Heading south on US-550 alongside the Uncompahgre River, the road skirts between mountains and hills at the entrance of the Uncompahgre National Forest. Here, the town of Ouray, named after the chief of the Utes, a Native American tribe who inhabited this region until they were driven out of the mountains by gold-greedy prospectors, is studded by curative hot springs. Take a dip to relish the therapeutic rewards of the Ouray Hot Springs Pool, said to promote good health, a great sex life and life-long youthful good looks.

Next it's onward to the magnificent 228-foot (70-metre) Clear Creek Falls in a rugged limestone gorge set within Box Canyon Falls Park on a rough dirt road – the bumps are worth it for views of the roaring cascades and bird-filled open meadows and forests. Continuing south on US-550 requires first-rate steering to navigate a series of tight hairpin bends as you enter the Million Dollar Highway. As a terrain peppered with millions of dollars of gold, silver and other precious minerals, and truly magnificent views, this cliff-hanging route takes you past creaking abandoned mines and through eerie mountain tunnels. Though it is richly endowed with beautiful scenery, the Million Dollar Highway is poorly equipped with guardrails, so resist the urge to fiddle with the in-car stereo or wing mirrors. Just when you dare blink, another roller-coaster switchback leads to another. Then, suddenly, it is the iron-rich sunburst-orange

Photo: Reinhard Schön

mountain peaks that make you draw breath: the depth of colour of this ragged ridge forms a striking feature against the golden shimmer of aspen leaves. Divine.

Follow the route over the Red Mountain Pass at an elevation of 11,018 feet (3,358 metres) – a neat divider between the Uncompahgre National Forest and the San Juan National Forest – before a dramatic descent through rounded valleys criss-crossed with woodland trails in a dazzling display of autumnal hues.

Silverton, a National Historical Site and former mining town renowned for its many Victorian buildings, is a fine example of a well-preserved Old West town. Silverton is remarkably well-preserved, having survived bar brawls, gold fever and heavy annual snowfall (typically 300 inches/762 centimetres each year), and avoided fire, unlike many similar mining settlements. A coal-fired steam train has served the route between nearby Durango and Silverton since 1881 and can still be enjoyed today. Or you can follow the Alpine Loop from Silverton to the Animas Forks ghost town, a windswept settlement weathered by time on the Animas River.

Back on the south-heading US-550 on a climbing stretch to the Molas Pass for sweeping views across Molas Lake, the route continues through hilly valleys backed by mountain peaks and forests of aspen, spruce, fir and ponderosa pine. The landscape slowly alters as you approach the town of Durango, set on a high desert plain tufted with cacti. It was this location, on the southern edge of the San Juan Mountains, that was picked for railroad development. By the 1880s, it had become a train hub and a centre of commerce and trade for fresh produce and minerals from the mines. Today, roadside farm stalls sell locally grown vegetables, fruit and the region's highly prized grass-fed meat and poultry (beef, pork, lamb, free-range chicken) as well as some unusual artisan cheeses. This fine agricultural outpost is also the start of the 469-mile (755-kilometre) Colorado Trail that runs all the way to Denver, winding its way through the peaks, lakes and creeks of the Colorado Rocky Mountains. In all, this beautifully maintained trail – built entirely by volunteer labour – passes through a half-dozen wilderness areas and eight mountain ranges, topping out at 13,271 feet (4,045 metres).

After Durango, you head west on US-160 through rolling hills for around 35 miles (56 kilometres) to reach the UNESCO World Cultural Heritage Site of Mesa Verde National Park, a striking ancient archaeological site of hundreds of cliff dwellings and thousands of artefacts and burial tombs built by the Anasazi people between AD 450 and 1300. The setting isn't just one of historical significance, but also an ethereal and peaceful location that offers plenty of time for peaceful contemplation as well as spellbinding views.

Push on west to Cortez on the US-160, then take CO-145 to Dolores, where you'll follow the Dolores River on a gradual climb back into the San Juan Mountains. Every guide book worth its salt will tell you to look for the layers of magma that formed the mountains at this point. For here is the route's famous Lizard Head Peak – an awkward 13,113-foot (3,997-metre) jutting volcanic spit. You get another chance to see it at the Lizard Head Peak Vista, though erosion is causing it to crumble. Pass Trout Lake on your left, on the descent as you free-fall into U-shaped valleys with the San Juan Mountains above. Follow the road and you'll spot signs for Telluride, a popular ski resort in winter and famous as the home of the very first bank Butch Cassidy robbed in 1889. If you're ready for a leg-stretch, you'll also see signs for the Keystone Gorge Trail.

Drive west along the San Miguel River through more deep-red cliffs and mountains to the San Miguel River Canyon – the point where the CO-145 joins the CO-62 to continue east. Enjoy more dazzling views of the peaks of the San Juan Mountains as the route ascends up and over the 8,970-foot (2,734-metre) Dallas Divide Mountain, then stop to drink in the views. Wow! Panoramas like these are good enough to imbibe. Once you've had your fill, it's time to descend to Ridgway where the San Juan Skyway Scenic Byway comes to an end.

The autumn colours along the San Juan Skyway are best seen mid-September to mid-October. If you can, do the drive in a 4×4 and take mountain bikes and walking boots with you – the wealth of leafy trails, camping huts and hiking routes make it a crime not to leave the car behind and get out on the beaten track. The Weehawken Trail along Camp Bird Road and the Full Moon Loop in Ironton Park are gorgeous in autumn with aspens on all of the cycle-friendly Ridgway Area Trails.

Contacts:
USA Tourism
www.visittheusa.com

PAN-AMERICAN HIGHWAY (TEXAS TO THE 'END OF THE WORLD' – USHUAIA, ARGENTINA)

Driving the Pan-American Highway is not for the faint-hearted. Even intrepid road-warriors develop a pathological hatred for their automotive on this gruelling trip, which is more than 18,000 miles long (over 28,900 kilometres).

This jaw-dropping mega-drive ploughs through the beating heart of twelve countries, from the USA to the southernmost point of South America. Conditions vary dramatically, from pockmarked trails through scrub-topped arid plains and sleek city freeways to roads through lush, green forest. On average, expect to barrel along at about 40 miles an hour if you're within the dim glow of a capital's outer suburbs. Rural stretches, however, are a law unto themselves. One minute you'll be weaving in and out of belching diesel trucks on a single-lane backroad before a swing of the wheel takes you on to the final curve of an eight-lane traffic-packed banana-shaped freeway before joining an empty country road as a solitary vehicle (passing one car an hour, generally head-on on the wrong side of the road).

Early morning, as daylight ascends, the only road companions will be massive earth-moving lorries that thunder off to unknown places. Pick up the route from Alaska, Canada or Texas to journey on the Pan-American Highway through Mexico, from Nuevo Laredo, Tamaulipas. Here, once the industrial buildings begin to thin out and give way to glades of trees, the air is laced with farmland smells: a mix of manure, grass and wet soil. A string of bland municipal buildings heralds the arrival of a built-up area: it's time to wave goodbye to the flame-coloured parrots of an extraordinary wilderness region and to say hello to the smog of Mexico City. Taxis and brightly painted buses rule the roads here – cross them at your peril. Grease and grime from traffic fumes turn into bitty platelets of dust and grit that cloud the windscreen.

Guatemala here we come! The journey beyond Guatemala City passes some bird-filled reed-bedded wetlands before entering El Salvador. Be prepared for regular roadblocks, security searches and ID checks on this stretch before crossing

into Honduras at El Amatillo past a riverbed, cracked like a broken egg. Border formalities take an age here, but you may be able to while away the time watching small boys shin up coconut trees with machetes almost as tall as themselves. Families of five or six squeak by on a clapped-out motorcycle. The potholes double in size once you approach Nicaragua, making it an unforgiving bum-bruising stretch. To avoid the biggest hollows, I pull the jeep from one side to the next like I'm riding a crazy slalom course. In these rain-soaked countries, newly laid asphalt doesn't last long and it's usual to rollick around on a rough gravel–mud mix. There are fewer trees here; much of the jungle has been lost to the chainsaw. Where the forest once stood, dark and thick, there is now flat patchy grass set with large, glassy puddles.

Once back on level land, it pays to give your jeep some TLC – I slosh a bucket of water over the windscreen and scrape off a sticky massacre of splattered flies. Now I'm ready to journey on to Costa Rica (via Managua). An hour from the border, I see my worst accident of the trip – an overloaded truck carrying plantain has crashed into a cow and the wreckage is blocking half the road. Cars are squeamishly inching around a bloodbath of entrails.

Lush, green rainforest and beach resorts characterise Costa Rica. By the time you've reached Panama at the Paso Canoas border, where the Pan-American Highway crosses the Panama Canal, the voyage has momentum. You, the car and the wide, open road. Which is why an abrupt, and rather premature, halt at the small Panamanian jungle town of Yaviza is something of a shock. For drivers, this gloomy outpost is literally the end of the road.

Though local people don't refer to the Darién jungle as 'the gap', the name given to it by outsiders rings true. The inaccessibility of this remote expanse is best appreciated from the sky. The thick sweep of dark green forms an unbroken barrier for miles and miles and miles – as far as the eye can see. Without roads, paths, cars, buses, coaches or tour buses, this area can only be traversed on foot, by horse or by primitive boat. You'll need a blade in hand to cut a path through the primeval tangles. It is hot, humid and energy-sapping. You will also need your wits about you as the human species is low-ranking here.

At more than 1.4 million acres (566,560 hectares), the Darién is five times the size of Los Angeles but is patrolled by fewer than a dozen rangers. They are paid a pittance to police, conserve, supervise and guard (no walkie-talkies, vehicles or GPS) thousands of species of plant, insects, and rare and endangered wildlife, remote ancient tribes and all manner of illicit activities, from drug-growing, smuggling and people trafficking to logging. For here in Darién's frontier town, set on a snaking caramel-coloured river, the Pan-American Highway is bisected by a 60-mile stretch of near-impenetrable jungle. On one side of this vine-knotted swathe is Panama. On the other, Colombia. To circumnavigate the 'gap' travellers must arrange the shipment of their vehicle by a cargo boat. Passengers can then enjoy a sailboat cruise from the east coast of Panama to Colombia's palm-hemmed Caribbean coast to be reunited with their car – an idyllic deviation around coral islands over sparkling waters that will delay them about a week.

Onward, the next step from Colombia is Ecuador – or you can opt for Venezuela (this is a prudent option if you're keen to keep fuel costs down). Then it's on to Peru, Chile and Argentina (via the capital Buenos Aires) to the city of Ushuaia in Tierra del Fuego, where untidy piles of second-hand tyres, bags of plantains and chopped wood are sold by the road. This trundling route is a favourite with rusty old trucks – but apart from one gasping its few last miles in front of me, the road is empty. I avoid a near-miss with a stray dog and a sinkhole the size of a minivan. Another branch of the highway heads from Buenos Aires to Paraguay, crossing into Asunción, but after 13,000 miles I'm keen to get out of the car and take a celebratory selfie with my station wagon. Then, I'm going to toast the trip with an ice-cold bottle of Quilmes beer.

Contacts:
Pan-American Highway website
www.go-panamerican.com

FLORIDA'S TAMIAMI TRAIL, USA

To reach the bottom of the Florida peninsula from Miami, it pays to reject the notion of doing a short, sharp dash along the four-lane Alligator Alley (I-75). For there is a more scenic two-lane trail full of great egrets, cypress trees and great Everglades scenery so close you can almost stick your hand out and touch it. The Tamiami Trail (US 41) offers glimpses of alligators gaping on sunny mud banks and a succession of picturesque roadside stops along the way. My Florida road-trip begins on Calle Ocho, the road that provides the sultry Latino heartbeat to Miami. I feast on bowls of *sancocho* (a hearty Panamanian soup) washed down with *jugo con agua* (freshly squeezed juice) and watch the elderly Cuban émigrés play dominoes at battered wooden tables on the sidewalk. All around me music blares out from basements, cafes and car stereos – Colombian salsa, Brazilian merengue and Panamanian cumbia. Bag-laden women chatter in machine-gun-pace Spanish while shopping for plantain, yucca and pinto beans; teens gather around the cell phone stalls. This is Miami's historic Latino community: a bustling Little Havana where Venezuelans, Chileans, Nicaraguans, Guatemalans, Colombians, Panamanians and Cubans, of course, can seek out essences of home.

The Tamiami Trail actually starts in the chichi stretch of road in upscale Bricknell Avenue – dubbed Millionaires Row with its penthouse loft apartments, designer delis and the sports car showrooms of the Financial District. Out on the trail, and heading for the wilderness, there is a sudden, peaceful calm that denotes you're around 20 miles (32 kilometres) west of downtown. The city is behind you with the road into the 'Glades shooting ahead of you. This is the country of the Miccosukee Indian, one of the many Native American peoples who once populated the peninsula. At the Miccosukee Indian Village, less than a half-hour from the boardrooms of Bricknell Avenue, you can be taught to wrestle an alligator by a young Miccosukee – an age-old tribal skill. The Miccosukee refer to the Everglades as 'the river of grass', a reference to the marshy, grassy waters of the wetlands. The tribe has a proud history, which pre-dates Columbus. The Miccosukee Indians were originally part of the Creek Nation, and then migrated to Florida before it became part of the USA. Today the tribe form part of a team of custodians of the 1.5-million-acre Everglades National Park, an area that protects the southern 20 per cent of the original Everglades.

Nearby, Shark Valley is one of the many entrances to the Everglades National Park and home to South Florida's most exciting cycle trails past alligators and wading birds. If you don't stop here, you'll no doubt want to take the Loop Road:

Photo: Ebyabe

a 26-mile (42-kilometre) side-trip along a historic gravel road, it winds through Big Cypress National Preserve, which for many years was Florida's version of the Wild West. Folk averse to law, societal rules and civilisation would descend here for its swing-door saloons, bar brawls and illicit liquor. Today, people travel Loop Road for a different kind of wild life for this off-the-beaten-track location is great for spotting alligators, birds, deer and even otter. Large scenic ponds are home to big populations of alligators and wading birds. Mysterious black swamps and thickly knotted cypress forests flank the road's edge through Big Cypress National Preserve's section of the Tamiami Trail. Designated as a scenic highway, this stretch is worth cruising slowly – alligators and otters cross the road not far from the abandoned Monroe Station. This historic building once served this remote stretch of road with gasoline and general provisions, but is now consigned to memories of the past. Continue to drive west to pass the Monument Lake campground on your right before reaching the Kirby Storter Boardwalk on your left. Stop here to stroll a magnificent half-mile of wooden boardwalk set over the leaves, creepers, grasses and wildlife of the cypress swamp: you'll be walking above snakes, alligators, otters, butterflies and birds.

A few more miles on and you'll spot a sign for the H.P. Williams Roadside Park, a scenic park with picnic tables and a viewing area where alligators and waders can be seen. From here, a dirt road leads north from the intersection where Turner River Road cuts through open prairies set along boggy canals – the wildlife here is phenomenal. Back on Tamiami, a half-mile west of Turner River Road, the Turner River Canoe Access is the boat launch site for wildlife-rich canoeing and the region's most popular paddling trail for good reason. Bring your own, or hire, and choose from kayaking trips upstream or downstream – the scenery is spectacular and the wildlife abundant. Another good trail departs a few miles west of here at Halfway Creek – look out for the sign by the Big Cypress Welcome Center. West of here, further along the Tamiami Trail, there is a nice little place to stop for lunch. Painted vermillion with a grey-topped roof, Joanie's Blue Crab Cafe has a slightly bizarre menu as befitting this funky old food joint, which dates back to 1928, the year the Tamiami Trail was completed. On the menu are frog legs, catfish, alligator, grouper and blue crab, which have all been caught locally. Located 36 miles (58 kilometres) west of Shark Valley, Joanie's is just a few miles from the Gulf Coast and is packed full of collectables, memorabilia and quirky bric-a-brac.

Just north on US 29 on the Tamiami Trail is the 2,000-feet (610-metre) Big Cypress Bend Boardwalk in the Fakahatchee Strand Preserve State Park. The boardwalk straddles a huge stretch of old-growth cypress swampland and it is a truly stunning place full of beautiful birds, butterflies and other wildlife. As the orchid and bromeliad capital of North America, Fakahatchee Strand Preserve State Park has 44 velvety native orchids and 14 native delicate bromeliad species. It's where the ghost orchid, topic of a book by Susan Orleans and a movie starring Meryl Streep, lives, along with the equally elusive Florida panther. Tawny brown on the back and pale grey underneath, the Florida panther is one of 32 *Puma concolor* subspecies known by many names – puma, cougar, mountain lion, painter, catamount and panther. These striking big cats once prowled and flourished in the South-East's woodlands and swamps, but suffered at the hands of European settlers in the 1600s. Habitat loss disrupted breeding and hunting and fear-driven panther persecution took root. Today, the panther is recognised as Florida's official state animal but is one of the most endangered mammals on Earth, with an estimated population of 100–180 in South Florida, the only known breeding population.

Before the Tamiami Trail reaches out for Marco Island, you pass Collier-Seminole State Park, established in 1947. As part of the Florida National Scenic Trail, the park has a 6.5-mile loop trail that is part-maintained by the Alligator Amblers of the Florida Trail Association. As a highly popular hiking trail that weaves around rivers, creeks and marshes, it also attracts legions of anglers, cyclists, canoeists and joggers. In recent years it has been part of an invasive plant eradication programme to remove all non-native flora. From Collier-Seminole State Park, the Tamiami Trail pushes on to the cities of Florida's Gulf Coast – Marco Island, Naples, Fort Myers, Sarasota, Bradenton and Tampa – leaving the wonders of the Everglades wilderness behind.

Contacts:
Florida Tourist Board
www.visitflorida.com

CANADA'S CABOT TRAIL

It has four bodies of water, clinging to its sides: the Atlantic Ocean, Bay of Fundy, Northumberland Strait and the Gulf of St Lawrence. And while I always struggle to pinpoint it on the map, it is actually larger then Denmark (though a little smaller than Scotland, after which it is named). Nova Scotia (meaning New Scotland in Latin) is a land inextricably linked to the sea – stand anywhere in this Canadian province and you'll never be far from the salty breezes, deep harbours and crashing waves of the coast. Of Nova Scotia's 950,000 population, more than 80 per cent claim Celtic ancestry. As the country's second-smallest province, with an area of 55,284 square kilometres (21,300 square miles), Nova Scotia comprises a chunk of mainland and a staggering 3,800 coastal isles. Many are as small as sprinkles, some no bigger than an executive car. The biggest, by far, is Cape Breton: a bird-shaped island to the north-east of the Nova Scotia mainland. This is where you'll find the world-renowned Cabot Trail: a favourite Canadian road-trip that consistently ranks high in *USA Today*'s 10 Best Motorcycle Trips, MSN Travel's 10 Most Underrated Attractions and *Zoomer*'s 7 Greatest Road Trips.

Looping for 298 kilometres (185 miles) around a sizeable chunk of Cape Breton Island, the Cabot Trail demands precision and accuracy from a driver. From a vehicle it requires top-notch brakes, for the route climbs through Cape Breton Highlands National Park at its northernmost extreme. This rugged flat-topped plateau cut by deep river valleys spans 951 square kilometres (367 square miles) and the Trail, at times, clings doggedly to the steepest ocean-facing cliffs. Home to moose, black bears and bald eagles, this raw wilderness transports you back to prehistoric times. Conifer-and-plant-munching prosauropod dinosaurs roamed this part of the Earth about 200 million years ago. In among the sprouting ferns, oversized peaks and dark forests of this most dramatic of upland landscapes, primeval spirits feel very much alive. Is that an echoing roar I hear deep in the valley, or just the surf at the coastline beyond?

In a straight run you could probably drive the Cabot Trail in around eight hours, but where's the fun in that? No, the Cabot Trail deserves at least twice that. Three times ideally, as it has a great deal to offer, from road-crossing bull moose

Photo: Padraic

in Bog, bald eagles in the tree tops by French Lake to rare wildflowers on spongey green plateau, including prey-catching pitcher plants and ghost-white orchids. The hardest decision is which way to drive it: a subject of great debate and conjecture in road-trip circles. Doing the trail clockwise is the only way to do it, some say. Counter clockwise is best, insist others. Me? Well, I don't think you can go wrong by tackling it from either direction, and if you've time, do both as they offer totally different views. Anti-clockwise allows you to drive snug to the guardrail while you climb up Smokey Mountain. Drive clockwise and you'll benefit from spectacular tight turns on the ride down. Either way, the Cabot Trail gives drivers the feeling that they are wholly at one with the road. Nature surrounds you, astounds and confounds you: a total thrill.

On the advice of a hotel owner, I head out clockwise, and I'm glad I did: there wasn't another car doing the loop my way so I had the trail to myself. Clockwise, I was told, offers the advantage of coffee at the Dancing Goat in Margaree. I would also hit Ingonish, where there's a great place for lunch, just after midday. I'm starting in Baddeck (there are actually four access points on the loop), which gives me some 'brain time' before 'my tyres hit the soil'. On Route 19 (Ceilidh Trail) I skirt along the coast past Mabou and Inverness, turning left at Dunvegan on Route 219. From here, shoot a left on to the bridge to follow the coast towards Cheticamp. Then turn right, to travel along the Margaree River towards Baddeck. There's a sign for the Cabot Trail just past Margaree Harbour. Swing a right here and you're on the Cabot Trail!

First, the roads are commendable: paved and well-signed. Once you've left the village of Baddeck behind (where Alexander Graham Bell, inventor of the telephone, made his home), the first sharp intake of breath you take is at the sight of the heavenly Bras d'Or Lake. I can already feel the car begin to climb on what will be a steady progression of hills as I pass the Gaelic College. If you feel in need of a good, strong cup of coffee, look out for Wreck Cove General Store (they also have maps and local information). On the hotel owner's advice, I had a double espresso before starting the long, slow engine-grinding climb up Smokey Mountain. From here, the Trail leads to Cape Smokey Provincial Park – I've been told to look out to sea for whales here but I feel pleased enough to spot eagles soaring overhead. I eat lunch by the Atlantic Ocean at Ingonish Beach, nestled in the Cape Breton Highlands in the company of a happy bunch of hikers who have just conquered lung-busting Skyline Trail. We swap takes of the pull of gradients, the clingy curves, the rise and fall of this tactile topography, agreeing it is one of the world's most striking coastlines. I am happy too.

With the sun on my face, and the engine purring like a kitten, the ocean views are almost dreamlike. Magnificent rivers cut through the rolling landscape: each broad sweep of upland is accented by a huge tree, farm building or crumbling relic. I stare down at the bay below and sense the powerful surge of the sea: it is almost magnetic. Fishing boats return with their haul of fish or with succulent lobster. Kayakers paddle past coastal rocks occupied by seals and seabirds. Bikes can be hired for the 92-kilometre (57-mile) Celtic Trail that weaves through Judique, Port Hood, Mabou and Inverness. With the keen eye of specialist wildlife guides, pods of Atlantic pilot whales can be spotted once they arrive here for summer to gorge on squid. There are also sport-fishing trips to catch tuna; puffin-spotting cruises to Bird Island and umpteen sailing charters. They all sound amazing. Me, I simply want to drive this road again.

Contacts:
Cabot Trail Tourism
www.cabottrail.com

SALAR DE UYUNI, BOLIVIA

Words defy even the most powerful literary pen when it
comes to describing Bolivia's Salar de Uyuni, the largest salt
lake on Earth at around 12,000 square kilometres (4,633
square miles). Set 3,600 metres (11,811 feet) above sea level,
this vast expanse is the result of the slow evaporation of a
prehistoric lake that vanished, leaving a barren, mineral-rich
moonscape terrain in its wake. Extraordinary geological
features give Salar de Uyuni an eerie, unearthly appearance
with spouting geysers, spurting hot springs and fumaroles
on a shimmering landscape tinged with crimson pink.
Located in the south-west of Bolivia, near the crest of the
Andes, the composition of the flats is mind-boggling with
high concentrations of halite and gypsum in a salt-crusted,
sun-bleached skeletal desert that has been cured by thin dry
mountain air.

Swept by high winds, the Salar de Uyuni looks a bit like
a cross between a Martian landscape and a Salvador Dali
painting. Pink flamingos wade through weirdly shaped
blood-red lagoons on a seemingly endless expanse of snow-
covered volcanoes, vast salt deposits and dried up lakes.
Cactus-hemmed pools are set below plum-purple, gust-
blown crags that leave explorers gasping for breath. Boasting
an extraordinary clarity, the deep blue of the altiplano sky is
often completely without cloud. Rocky plateaus form a fringe

around views that are nothing less than staggering amid a bubble of sulphuric suds and frosted peaks and troughs. Eroded crags and chasms litter the parched-pink landscape where brackish steaming funnels emit a turbine-like roar. Gurgling mud pools hide among fiery-red canyons close to algae-rich waters that trickle along wind-chafed rocky subterranean fissures seemingly sprinkled with whitewash. Rough trails weave precariously around fossilised lake sediments enriched by fragments of coral and limestone to magmatic stretches high above brine puddles and irregularly shaped boulders. At sunrise, gentle wisps of smoke puff into the pastel glow as flamingos study their reflections in the moisture – a mind-blowing vision in this serene other-world.

If the imagery is surreal, then it is an equal match to the Salar de Uyuni's history. For the unusual geological formations here in Bolivia's south-west make it one of the driest, strangest places on Earth. There is space, a lot of space, on these wild, expansive salt plains. In fact Earth observation satellites use its surface to calibrate their altitude and global positioning systems. That's how big it is. According to fossil records, the salt flats were part of prehistoric Lake Minchin more than 30,000 years ago. Standing 3,656 metres (11,995 feet) above sea level, Lake Minchin would've competed with Lake Titicaca for highest lake in the world, but it dried up thousands of years ago, leaving behind the flat concentration of salt we see today. Here you walk over old corals that were once home to prehistoric lake creatures and stand among giant cacti that grow one metre per century in a salt plain that covers 10,360 square kilometres (4,000 square miles). Ravines of salt accentuate the beauty of large reservoirs of lithium-rich brine. In fact, approximately 70 per cent of the world's lithium reserves are found in Salar de Uyuni – an extraordinary resource.

Photo: Entropy1963

From La Paz, it is a 570-kilometre drive to the village of Uyuni on a mix of paved and roughshod roads: the first 230 kilometres to Oruro are quite good, but the last 340 kilometres are pretty shocking. Time your journey into the Salar de Uyuni to arrive in the early morning when the air is frigid and cool. Though you may need to crank the heater up in your car as you wait for the sun to fully awaken, it will be hot enough to crack the skin on your forehead within a few hours of entering the Salar de Uyuni. Press your palm to your brow and your hands will feel as rough as sand paper. The sun sizzles your shoulders on even the shortest stroll. Cover up with loose-fitting clothing, wear a hat and slather on plenty of sunscreen. If you can't set off early to arrive at Salar de Uyuni for sunrise, try to arrive late afternoon and stay for the sunset. As shadows grow long and the egg-yolk sun begins to dip low on the horizon, shimmering bands of tangerine orange, deep purple and golden yellow dominate the sky. Reflecting gorgeous colours, the silvery surface of the salt plains seems to transform into coloured crystals – a mystical and hallucinogenic encounter with the different minerals created by runoff from the surrounding mountains and filtered by the glowing light.

Containing an estimated 10 billion ton of salt, with no drainage outlets, this high-salinity basin is rich in the legend of the Bolivian Aymara people. According to ancient tribal belief, the mountains surrounding the salt plains were once giant people. When a cruel infidelity was discovered, with one giant betrayed for another, the resulting tears of pain and despair are said to have flowed in a vast rocky dip and created the salt flats. Today some enterprising local folk have built salt-brick accommodation for travellers visiting the Salar de Uyuni. Simple buildings made from rustic bricks of cemented salt contain furniture and amenities crafted from salt blocks – an admirable display of ingenuity. Simply knock at the door to book a salt-built room – they are available at a shoe-string rate.

Contacts:
Bolivia Tourism
www.bolivia.travel

HISTORIC COLUMBIA RIVER HIGHWAY SCENIC BYWAY, USA

If you are merely attempting to cross the Columbia Gorge, you'd take the utilitarian I-84: the fastest and easiest cut-through from A to B. But if you want to traverse the road while surrounded by mesmerising scenery, at a more leisurely pace, you will seek out the Historic Columbia River Highway Scenic Byway. Beginning 16 miles (26 kilometres) to the east of downtown Portland and ending at former Native American trading post The Dalles, this magnificently engineered trail opened in 1915 to allow access to one of the most beautiful, exciting and diversely scenic locations in the Pacific North-West. Today thousands of road-trippers buckle up and set off to discover the natural splendour of the terrain around the Gorge via the Historic Columbia River Highway (Highway 30). Many arrive on the route from Troutdale (Exit 17 on I-84) and cross the Troutdale Bridge before screeching to a halt at the edge of the Sandy River and gasping at the views. This is where all of the finest sweeping shots of the Gorge have been snapped over time – for magazines, travel books and advertising. Stand here to capture the moment (and the view) for posterity and you'll also have your first encounter with the legendary Columbia Gorge winds: mega-gusts formed from atmospheric pressure around the waterfalls that create a wind-tunnel effect. As one of the windiest places in America's North-West, the combination of strong winds and river currents provides excellent windsurfing conditions in the Gorge. In the coldest months, freezing rain is a common hazard, while in warmer dry periods severe turbulence can see wind-speeds reach 105 miles (169 kilometres) an hour.

There is a seemingly endless succession of tumbling waterfalls in the Gorge area (over 90 on the Oregon side alone) in rock strata dating back to the Miocene period (12–17 million years ago). Evidence suggests other parts of the Gorge's geology were shaped during the Pleistocene period (700,000–2 million years ago). Lands and river courses shifted during the forming of the Cascade Range: the original location of the Columbia River's delta was around 100 miles (161 kilometres) south of where it is now. At the end of the last Ice Age, erosion cut steep dramatic walls exposing many layers of volcanic rock. The Gorge has also supported human life for more than 13,000 years, through food, transportation and irrigation. In among the jagged cliffs, the Columbia Gorge, with its wide range of elevations and microclimates, is also home to more species of flowering plants than any other region in the Pacific North-West – almost 750 at last tally.

The route winds through densely wooded expanses and past pounding waterfalls shrouded in a cool, damp spritz. Journey on and you'll come to America's fourth-highest cascades, Multnomah Falls. Park by a fine old stone-built lodge that now doubles as a cafe and info centre, and follow the neatly paved, steep trail that reaches up 620 feet

(189 metres) to the very top of the Falls – the fine spray is oh-so-refreshing as it hits the skin. As the largest and most famous waterfall along the historic highway, this is also the state's most visited natural attraction – part way up, there is a picturesque arched bridge that is directly in front of the Falls. Above the Falls, other trails lead off into Mount Hood National Forest.

Continue east for a couple of miles to Oneonta Gorge, a thin rift in the cliffs set close to the world-class collection of brightly coloured flora at Oneonta Botanical Area. Continue a half-mile beyond to arrive at Horsetail Falls about a half-hour drive from Bonneville Dam, where staff run free tours (9am to 5pm). There's also a fish-viewing room and hatchery. A few miles on you'll find the trailhead that leads to Wahclella Falls, where enormous dark-brown boulders are stained lime-green by lichen. Yet it's Eagle Creek that attracts the greatest number of walkers, as the most popular trail in the Gorge. This is the trail to follow if you only have time for one hike in the Gorge to see its mossy trailing boughs, sprouting bushes, zigzag stone trails, fish-filled rivers, springtime blossoms, wildflowers and ancient burial sites steeped in tales of traders, hunters and settlers.

Not far beyond Eagle Creek is the Bridge of the Gods, which connects Oregon and Washington at the site where there once stood a natural bridge used by the gods, according to local legend. Just beyond the Bridge of the Gods is Cascade Locks. Completed in 1896, the locks enabled steamships to pass unhindered, although the opening of the Columbia River Scenic Highway in 1915 made the trip even easier by land. Visitors can watch the fish as they pass underwater windows and there is also an adjacent hatchery where trout, salmon and steelhead are raised before being released. Two small museums at the Locks narrate the history of the

Photo: Tony Webster

region, the Cascade Locks Historical Museum (in the old lock tender's house) and the Port of Cascade Locks Visitors Center, which is also the ticket office for a two-hour cruise on sternwheeler *Columbia Gorge*.

Any way you look at it, the Historic Columbia River Highway Scenic Byway is an absolute marvel: for its visionary engineering, jaw-dropping scenery and rich history. One of the greatest engineering feats of the modern age, its engineer, Samuel C. Lancaster, did 'not [want] to mar what God had put there' and worked diligently to make full use of this magnificent natural canvas. At 80 miles (129 kilometres) long and up to 4,000 feet (1,219 metres) deep, the result is the only sea-level route through the Cascade Mountain Range. Lancaster carved the road through lava and basalt to create a route of constantly changing perspectives. He protected, showcased and honoured a landscape rich in cultural history as an important place for the many indigenous peoples of the Columbia Basin and part of the Oregon pioneers' trail. Today, the Historic Columbia River Highway Scenic Byway is a National Historic Civil Engineering Landmark that includes 23 unique bridges. As one of America's 'Most Scenic Drives', driving its length is a magnificent way to spend five hours.

Contacts:
Columbia River Highway Scenic Byway, USA
www.columbiariverhighway.com

NOTES

NOTES

NOTES

Also available

PETER
PUGH

MOST INFLUENTIAL
BRITONS
OF THE LAST 100 YEARS

ISBN: 9781785780349 (paperback) / 9781785780356 (ebook)

IN ASSOCIATION WITH
TIMPSON

Also available

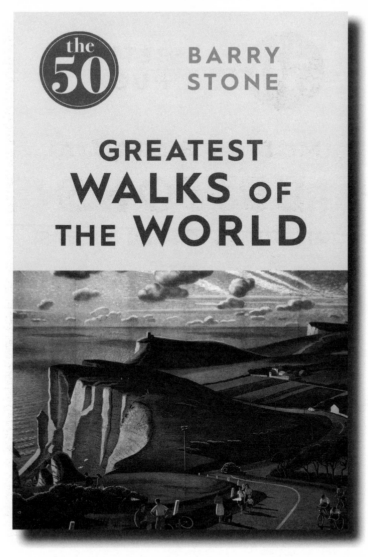

the 50

BARRY
STONE

GREATEST
WALKS OF
THE **WORLD**

ISBN: 9781785780639 (paperback) / 9781785780646 (ebook)

IN ASSOCIATION WITH
TIMPSON

Also available

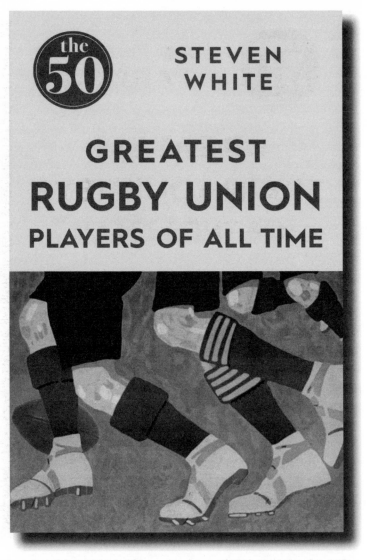

ISBN: 9781785780264 (paperback) / 9781785780271 (ebook)

IN ASSOCIATION WITH
TIMPSON

Also available

ANTHONY
LAMBERT

GREATEST
TRAIN JOURNEYS
OF THE WORLD

ISBN: 9781785780653 (paperback) / 97817857880660 (ebook)

IN ASSOCIATION WITH
TIMPSON